The Miracle
of Energy

by

Mohammad Mehdi Dousti

Published by:
Gulf Book Service Ltd
20-22 Wenlock Road, London.
NI 7GU
UK
Email: info@gulfbooks.co.uk

ISBN: 978-1-7384322-3-3
Year: February 2024 Edition 2
Cover Design: Razia Hoshiary Fard

Table of Contents

Introduction

I do not consider myself a motivational speaker, nor am I someone who writes books about success. I did not write this book with the sole purpose of adding another title to the list of success books. I wrote this book because I felt responsible for everyone who sought to follow the paths of growth and prosperity in business but did not know how, where, or when to start. Unfortunately, there aren't many instances of successful businesses in modern culture.

Due to this, and other reasons, most people, especially the younger generation, do not see a straightforward and clear path toward success. Most of them assume that if they want to make money, they must gain from the so-called nepotism, favouritism, patronage, or similar means, or they should just give up. Then, they conclude that they should not waste their youthful energy or that they should abort their country. In some cases, they try to work together; however, they stop after encountering the first obstacle.

I think these negative and limiting attitudes can change through cultural work, promoting localised ways of success, and offering young people correct and positive role models. This will help them realise they can be successful even at a young age if they work hard, do not give up, and know what works.

I have always hoped all the young people would do well in business so that we could all work together to make the world a happier and more beautiful place.

The book you are holding is not the book of success principles!

You have probably seen these titles on the covers of the countless books about success that are available in bookstores, you have likely encountered these titles: 5 Guidelines for Success Ten things that successful people do! Twenty practices successful people follow. Interestingly, it takes less time for successful people to write books on their own achievement. Often, it is other people that look at their lives and try to figure out what has made them successful. They then combine these algorithms with their own perceptions to present a universally applicable version to the audience. Mostly, none of these techniques or versions often satisfy everyone.

In fact, energetic people are the successful ones. It does not matter what time they wake up every day— whether it is 5 a.m. or 12 p.m. However, the majority of the books that have been published about them fail to even acknowledge their high level of energy. Instead, they focus on other things. They, for instance, get up early, study, etc. Because energy is the most important factor and everything else is merely incidental, no one will ever succeed by replicating tiny things.

Have you ever felt like you needed to get started on something, but you put it off for a long time and did not eventually do it? Have you ever had a great idea but did not work on it, and then you found out that someone else did the same thing? Have you ever thought, "I wish I had seized the opportunity when I was younger"?

I have read a lot of books on success, so I am not going to repeat what has already been said. I think each person's principles and techniques for life and business are different from those of others, and that each person should find their own techniques based on their biological conditions and characteristics.

So, based on my work path and my experiences, I hope to provide my readers with a "fresh perspective and attitude" in this book. In any manner, I don't want to keep using the same old adages and prejudices. I hope this book will enable you to view things differently, because I am aware that one person's thoughts do not necessarily apply to everyone.

A person's knowledge of the numerous facets of life comes from their particular life experiences. Knowing the outcomes and attitudes that result from these experiences aids in self-analysis, self-discovery, and character identification.

Not all roads lead to Rome!

The current dominant culture encourages people to study as far as they can in school. However, do all people have the same talents and interests, and should they all be told and forced to follow the same path?

In today's world, many people believe that education is the key to success. Nobody inquires about your new work, your new skills, the chances you've taken, when you've gotten up after falling, or your level of happiness.

No one says that the first step of doing everything is to fail.

The over-emphasis on studying has broken the link between working hard and getting good results. A young person who has not gone to college thinks that he or she is not successful. This makes them lose all their energy. When young people go to college, they see many people who have spent their whole lives in college still do not have jobs. So, what reasons are left for them to choose or stay on this path that has already been set? They want to get a new job, and their family expects them just to study. The youth and their families start a persistent struggle, which drains the energy of both sides. In the middle of these constant struggles, the original and most important issue - energy - is lost.

In the world we are living in, having a degree is not as important as being skilled at practical tasks. Modern life has pushed society in a direction where people with communication, behavioural, social, and interdisciplinary skills are needed much more than they were in the past. The most prestigious schools in the world are addressing this issue in their curricula. However, most successful people still criticise the education systems that are in place. Thus, the worst way to define effort is to tell people what they should try. No one can choose the best way for someone else.

Is it not the case that any single person is created to perform a special job? Why does everyone need to go to college? People have different talents, skills, and interests. One of them can be a good cook, and the other one can be a good welder. When I realised that the university was not going to help me get to where I wanted to go, I dropped the course and left the university in the last semester to find a different way to fulfill my dreams. This way tells people to have energy, take risks, and move on. No one will tell you what to do because you already know that.

You might think that when I left college and started down a new, unknown path, I was on the road to progress and success. However, that was not the case. My path was full of mistakes, failures and goals I did not achieve, just like the paths of everyone else who steps into the unknown and the dangerous. As I write these words, I am working to solve the problems and challenges that lie ahead, and I am fighting to reach my goals.

What is the Energy Book about?

The issue of energy is not just an interesting idea; it comes from the deepest parts of who we are. Energy is a precious gift that makes us want to move and tells us to try to live better. We need energy to be able to think, learn, gain experience, and move on. Energy enables us to take risks, and when we fail, it tells us to get back up and try again.

When I started my business, I was twenty-three years old. I was too young and inexperienced to take on this job. I did not know how to do the work because I did not have the right knowledge and skills, but something inside me caused me to move on. I call it "internal energy". At that age, the only thing I had going for me was energy. Vibrant energy is not about being happy or moving around. Instead, it is something in the inner and deeper parts of who we are. For instance, a young man with a lot of inner force will make significant business decisions that will result in enormous success. The energy is something that picks up the boxer lying in the corner of the ring so that he may not lose the match.

When I was writing this book, my friends frequently questioned me on why I was writing about energy. As the topic has a lot of scientific and theoretical roots, they would ask me, "Don't you worry about the scientific level of your book?"

The answer was simple: "Follow competitions between teens at schools or in other places. They have not been taught how to work as a team, and they do not know what it takes to be successful. They get together on their own and work well as a team because they have a lot of energy."

I am not going to write a book on energy. It is something that psychologists have dealt with sufficiently. This book is about how I think about energy and what I know about it; I want to say that energy is something that stays. You can find your way when you have energy. Energy never deceives you. If you spend it somewhere, it will show up somewhere else in a different way. Energy is always around us and stays with us. We should know about it and take care of it.

This book is about the amazing force that makes a child get back up after falling over and try again until they learn to walk. It is the same force that gives the silkworm the power to break out of its cocoon and fly around the world like a beautiful butterfly. "The Magic of Energy" gives you the kind of energy that you cannot get anywhere else. It is the kind of energy that makes you a hero and shapes your life's adventures. Energy is a magical power that lasts forever and is the most important thing about us that we need to understand and use.

When you read "The Magic of Energy," you'll realise that you have a vast world inside of you and that you own a limitless supply of power that is inextricably linked to the energy of existence. Your energy joins the energies that gave life to the book when you read these lines. This indicates that you have been picked to go closer to excellence, growth, and progress. Don't pass up this once-in-a-lifetime opportunity or this miracle of life. Pay attention to your feelings once you finish the book, and do not put off today's work until tomorrow. "The Magic of

Energy" challenges readers to reflect after each chapter and to take action at the conclusion.

The heroes always leap into the dark, where they face dangers on paths they do not know and have to be strong to get to the magical land of happiness. If you take a brave step on this journey, happy endings are always there for you. When this book was written or rewritten, it was this energy that kept saying, *"Write me!"*

Mohammad Mehdi Dousti

Chapter One: What is Energy?

Energy magician

Energy Always exists

Energy Bank

Work and Energy Equation

How is energy made?

Energy should be organized

Managing energy or time?

Energy management tools

Study yourself to reach self-awareness

Now you're in charge of yourself

I know it won't happen!

You are sitting in your room. You have not done anything special, and nothing has happened; nevertheless, you do not even feel like getting up!

Today, you were supposed to hang out with your friends and have fun, but now you do not feel like moving, let alone going to the forest park, and you do not feel like seeing anyone. You feel like there is nothing in your body; you are like an entirely discharged cell phone battery. Nothing can charge your battery!

What are you empty of?

Your sister comes up to you and says, "If you don't have anything else to do, can you help me with my math homework?"

You shrug and say, "I don't even want to hang out with my friends today, let alone figure out math problems!"

Sitting next to you, your sister asks, "Is there something wrong? Are you not feeling well? You felt good yesterday."

You answer confusedly, "Nothing is wrong; I just don't have the energy."

You used the word "energy" in your speech, but you did not mean it in a scientific way at all.

Yes, we do use this word a lot in our everyday lives and in business to let people know how we feel.

"Why?" asks your sister. "Yesterday, you were so energetic!"

What do you and your sister mean when you talk about energy? I am sure you are talking about how you feel about something. You are talking about the same thing, which is how we move through life. No one needs to know anything about psychology in order to talk about this energy. We deal with it every day. It is both outside and inside of us - but sometimes, it gets stronger or weaker, does not show up the way we expect, or shows up in a different way.

We are always dealing with this energy.

Energy magician

We have heard a million times that a human being has a body and a soul. We have always known what this means: that our lives are made up of physical and spiritual parts. We can see and touch the physical part, and our five senses are the main tools used by the physical part, but the spiritual part is hidden inside us; some people call it the mind, while others have given it other names, like spirit and soul. However, what all such definitions have in common is that they refer to something inside us. This part of our lives that is not made of matter is like a huge forest where the powerful magician is hidden. A magician who has control over our internal energy and can use it to do anything. We have to find him and ask him to use his magic power. To do this, we have to go on a journey and get to the core of that dense forest. However, we cannot find this magician without a map.

Like a treasure map, this book shows you how to go deep into the inner forest to find your energy magician. Then, he will use his magic words to make your energy flow so that the results of your work will always surprise you.

The tools of magicians are a flying broom, a magic wand, an invisibility cloak, and magic words; the energy magician also has his own tools. The energy spell will help you if you know how the tools work and take care of them all the time. You will learn about the energy magician's tools and the manner of using them chapter by chapter. The Energy Book turns on the magic of energy by calling and introducing the energy-givers. It also helps the energy magician create a safe environment by calling the energy-drainers and giving advice on how to deal with them.

Energy Always exists

The energy magician has just one rule, which is easy to remember:

The Law of Conservation of Energy

The law of conservation of energy states that energy can neither be created nor destroyed but it is only transformed from one form to another. For example, electricity can be changed into heat energy, light energy, and sound energy. The conversion of sound energy into electrical energy, the conversion of light energy into chemical energy in processes like photosynthesis in green plants, and many other examples are observed every day.

When the energy magician talks about the law of energy conservation, he is referring to something inside of us that is connected to the surrounding world. The law of energy conservation says that when we use our own energy to do something, we have only used it in a way, whether we get the results we want or not. This energy that is used up does not just go away. It comes back to us somewhere else and is used again. You put your energy into a certain subject or task, and when it is needed, this energy will come back to you in another place without being even slightly wasted or annihilated, even if you do not know where or why it is sent back to you.

Energy Bank

You have worked hard to get ready for the badminton match, and you go in hoping to win. When you do not, you feel like a failure. "Why?" asks your friend. "You deserved better!"

You say, "I don't know. To be honest, I practiced a lot for this match and put a lot of effort into it. You are aware of my efforts, though ... I feel like all my energy is wasted."

Do not be mistaken. Your effort did not go to waste, but it did not get you what you wanted. Instead, it turned into something else. You have an energy bank inside you that you can use in different ways and places.

Work and Energy Equation

The badminton tournament moves on to the second round. This time, you try harder than before. You definitely want to win this time! Every day, you practice for hours and hours, and by the end of the day, you are so tired that you become unconscious. Yet, in the morning, you wake up ebullient and energetic, ready to practice again. Such physical fatigue does not reduce your internal energy.

When some of your friends see how hard you work, they ask, "Didn't you get tired of practicing? Doesn't matter! Your opponent is very robust."

Or, they ask, "Oh, where do you get so much energy that you never get tired?" Let's linger here for a moment!

Your friends also used "energy" to understand what was going on with you.

You reply, "Tired?" as you puff and sweat. "No, I have no reason to be tired. By the way, it feels very good!"

The closer the competition day gets, the harder you practice. Each workout gives you energy and motivation to approach the competition. Your friends would only see you sweating, blushing, and gasping for breath and assume you were just wasting your energy.

They are not wrong, of course. The more you work out, the more physical energy you lose. Do you know what was their mistake? Your friends followed the physical equation of work and energy, but you followed the energy magician's rules.

In physics, the equation for work and energy states that "Work equals the energy used." This means that the harder you work, the more energy you use. Consider a charging toy car, for this car to move, it needs to use battery energy. Now, let's say that turning the wheels of the toy car does not use energy, but instead, charges the battery. The energy magician's view about work and energy is exactly the same: "Working does not use up your internal energy; on the contrary, it can increase it. In other words, the level of internal energy goes up while you are working."

When you finish something and get the result you wanted, your internal energy soars. Even when going through the job, you gain energy! It is the energy that gives you the ability to keep going. *If we have a lot of internal energy, we can do more than what our bodies can handle.*

Imagine a woman who is not a good athlete and does not have any special physical skills. If someone stronger than her hurts her child, she will roar like a lion and attack to protect the child. When a person meets a wolf in the woods, they are so full of energy that they ignore their physical weakness or run away faster than they ever could. In both cases, the internal energy has boosted the physical energy. *The more internal, the stronger the energy.*

The energy magician's equation does not match up with the physical equation of work and energy!

The energy magician shows the other side of the coin: He says that even though physical activities use a lot of energy, they can increase internal energy. Then, the internal energy can make up for physical weakness so that we can become readier to work.

My sister, an artist, typically gets very upset when she follows her religion's rules about fasting in her everyday life. Hunger and thirst make her weak and throw off the balance of her life, but when she stands in front of a blank canvas and picks up a paintbrush, she gets so lost in the world of shapes and colors that she does not remember anything. She sometimes spends the whole day in her studio painting and making up scenes from her dreams. How does she have so much energy that she forgets to eat and drink?

This is an example of countless experiences that we all go through in different ways and different situations.

How is energy made?

The human mind is like a factory that produces our internal energy. The mind's raw materials for making energy products are the many bits of information that are constantly and unconsciously put into the brain through the five senses. The human brain cannot accept the countless input data, so it prioritizes them and removes the extra ones.

However, how do these numbers turn into power? In our minds, our beliefs shape how we think about environmental facts. The belief filter chooses what input data should be sent to the brain. Then, the brain takes all of these pieces of information and analyzes them using the person's attitude. This is how internal energy is made.

Three steps make up the simple model of how energy is made:

1. Getting a lot of data, filtering them through the filter of beliefs, and sending them to the brain.
2. Processing and analysing the filtered data in the brain (the energy-producing factor).
3. Producing and storing the energy.

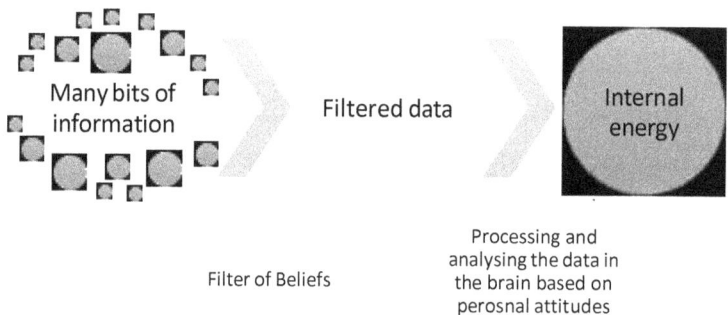

Many bits of information

Filter of Beliefs

Filtered data

Internal energy

Processing and analysing the data in the brain based on perosnal attitudes

It is true that the filter of beliefs keeps the brain from being overloaded with information by choosing what data to pay attention to and what to ignore. However, a problem may occur when we do not have positive beliefs. For example, if a person thinks that where they live does not give them a chance to get ahead, the filter of their beliefs will remove all data and inputs that contain opportunities and keep them from getting into their minds.

Why do some people work hard but still do not make much money? That is because, based on the filter of beliefs, they believe they cannot become rich.

The brain processes and analyses the information that gets through the filter of beliefs and turns it into energy. Every thought and feeling has its own energy. The more positive and optimistic a mind is about how things are, the better it can take advantage of opportunities and turn every problem and setback into a chance to reach its goals. In other words, you can also generate energy from negative inputs.

Are your beliefs making it hard for you to see opportunities and let go of useful information? How will the energy needed to move be made if this process does not produce energy as much as possible? If you do not like how your life turned out or did not get what you wanted, look at your beliefs, attitudes, and the energy that came from your thoughts. How do you feel about problems in life?

Any change in the way people think can change how they act and how they look at data. This can lead to the optimal use of energy. In general, being able to make energy from thoughts and beliefs means that you can still make good energy even if you do not receive good raw materials or data from the environment.

Internal energies are related to our mental analysis.

Energies should be integrated

If you have watched the movie "Harry Potter and Hogwarts School of Witchcraft and Wizardry", you know the powerful headmaster of Hogwarts. A school where all the girls and boys have magical powers but do not know what they can do or when, where, or how to use them.

Now that you have found your inner magician, how well do you know its powers, and how do you use them? Do you know where and when to use these skills?

Your energy magician needs a manager to organise the energies and teach when, where, for what, and to whom to use each word so that you may know how to take control of the energies you are connected to.

Be the manager of your energy magician

By planning how you use your time and energy, you can improve how well you do your work and keep it from going to waste. When you know how to organise your energies well, it is easy to figure out what gives you energy and what drains it. Then, you can do things to boost the energy-givers and try to get away from the energy-drainers. By channelling the energies of the magician within you, you will protect yourself from the energy-drainers that are consuming such magician abilities.

Before starting energy management, take a look at your current state and see if you want to change it into a better one.

A good manager always knows what is going on with the people he or she is in charge of. You should also pay attention to yourself with sharp eyes and senses.

Managing energy or time?

To use the energy magician's skills, you must be able to manage him. You have two options: "management of time" to use your energy or "management of energy" to use your time. *Which option do you prefer?*

Make a list of tasks you should do. Set the starting and end of the tasks. Can you stay loyal to them? If something important comes up, these plans will all have to be changed. Sometimes, you do not feel like doing something, other times, you do not have the energy to do something. Such situation implies that you are not able to manage your time!

Aging, greying of hair, and the emergence of wrinkles are good examples that make the passage of time felt. Changes in the seasons and the growth of trees are also signs that time is going by. Time is never available to us, but we worry about managing it and forget that the only thing we can manage is our energy. We cannot control time or even prevent it from passing, but we are constantly concerned about managing it.

Energy management aims to keep your energy levels constantly high and your batteries charged. What would happen if you manage your energy instead of time, which is not under your control?

You will most probably know people who continue to work energetically even at the age of seventy. The passage of time is evident in their hair, face, and their shaking hands, but they continue to work energetically. Being on the slopes of life and having physical disabilities do not prevent them from being energetic.

There are also young people who do not study, work, or do anything else out of the ordinary. Whenever they are asked why they are not doing anything, they say they are bored or do not feel like it, and in this way, they waste days and nights and miss opportunities.

If you want to use your time effectively, you need to have a lot of energy, because then, you can take the time under control. This means that if you have a lot of energy, you spend less time doing things.

In some stories, the protagonists find themselves in a situation that makes them realise they only have one day left to live. These stories depict the actions and reactions of these characters in such difficult circumstances and show how they try to make the most of their remaining time. In these kinds of stories, the main characters know that they cannot control time, so they choose to manage their energy instead. Managing energy shows how they keep their energy levels high, which gives them the ability to do more work in less time. These types of stories illustrate the relationship between energy and time very well. They show that the more energy you have, the better you can use time, and that it can even change how you see the time passing. Your sense of time depends totally on how much energy you have. This is another strange rule of the energy magician. If you are tired and bored when you do something, time will move slowly and be hard for you to keep up with. On the other hand, if you are full of energy, you will not notice that time is passing, and you might even think that the day went by in a flash. In both cases, the time has not changed, but how you feel about time has changed based on your feelings.

Your sense of time is completely affected by your energy level.

Energy management tools

For energy management, you need to be aware of your energy levels and know about energy-givers and energy-drainers. In order to use your internal energies, you must be able to recognise them. Knowing the internal energies helps you to take advantage of them by recognising their level, condition, and type, or identifying and eliminating any factor that lowers the level of constructive energies.

Study yourself to reach self-awareness

You are like a book that only you can open and read. This book is like a treasure map: when you open it, the words appear and become readable. This book has two main parts: the body and the mind.

The parts of this book have already been written by you in the path of your life. By reading it, you will gain self-awareness and you can continue to write this book as you like.

When you reach self-awareness, you are ready to know your energy-givers and energy-drainers. Once you know what they are, you can work to make one stronger and get rid of the other. You must be telling yourself that it is obvious that success, happiness, money, a good job, good grades, a promotion, and a high status all give you energy. You do not have to know such things, but it might be interesting to know that this is not always the case!

Sometimes, energy-givers are things we do not even think about, including getting started, taking risks, failing, tolerating, being open to new ideas, taking small steps, etc. Have you ever looked at these things as energy-givers?

Now you are the manager of yourself

If you can pay attention to yourself, you will find energies that are unique to you. Some people get started by watching a funny movie, others by listening to music, and still others by walking in the woods or by the sea.

We often feel like we need someone to come and give us energy. Family, friends, and many other things outside of us can give us energy, but the main source of energy is inside of us, and the energy is stronger the more internal it is.

A group of people see their job as the only way to make money. People like these just think about the end of the month and their salary, overtime, bonuses, and welfare. They write down the number of their deductions, and for half of the next month, they protest and become grumpy because of working ten hours less overtime than the previous month. They are driven by things outside of themselves and need the energy to do their jobs. They keep working because they do not want to lose their salary.

If such people find themselves in a difficult working situation, they will lose their job in some way, and if there is a problem with their income, they will completely stop working.

There are also other types of people who get their energy from the inside. They stick to their work process until they achieve their goals under any circumstances, and as they progress, they gain more strength and energy in such a way that they grow at least twice their current position in less than five years. Their income is not the same as the first group, of course.

A person's internal energy is part of who they are. If we get our energy from ourselves, we do not get hurt by being in the wrong place; although, we should not let anyone from the outside world steal our energy.

When our energy is internal, nothing or no one can take us off our paths. Socrates, the prominent Greek philosopher, was ridiculed by his friends, acquaintances, and neighbours because of his ideas and thoughts. Even his wife made fun of him and put him down. However, he used his internal energy to think, organise, and proceed with his work while no one from the outside could stop him from thinking and planning. He constituted the cornerstone of western philosophy by relying on his own internal energy. Today, we do not know the name of Socrates' wife or any of his neighbours or friends. They are an army lost in the depths of time, and not even the dust of their bodies remain. However, the name of Socrates shines at the forefront of Western philosophy. His internal energy has always moved through the world, and it still does.

Keep our internal energy safe.

I know it won't happen!

Do you remember the cartoon about Gulliver? Glam, a character in the land of Lilliput, used to be negative and pessimistic all the time. His famous line was, "I know it won't happen." Because their minds were clear and active, Gulliver and his friends never paid attention to what he said. They did things to solve the problems, and the Glam's predictions always proved wrong; in the end, Gulliver and his friends would succeed.

The biggest difference between Gulliver and his friends was in their attitudes toward the events and their abilities.

Now, you know an energy magician, you are familiar with the importance of energy management, and you know that you need energy sources to make the magic of the internal magician perform his duties well. Is it the case that you do not know where energy comes from? Do not be afraid! You have access to these things! There are many ways to get energy.

The main source of energy is your mind and attitude, which are also the source of the energy magician's power. If the magician gets the energy he needs from a healthy source, the product is also safe. The more positive and optimistic your thoughts and feelings are, the more constructive energy will be given to you by the magician.

Chapter Two: Energy Scan

Energy detective

Energy Scan

Energy drainers

Don't be a blindfold horse

Black hole, a major energy-drainer

How are energy black holes made?

Black Hole Monster

How can energy black holes be stopped?

Threatening energy drainers

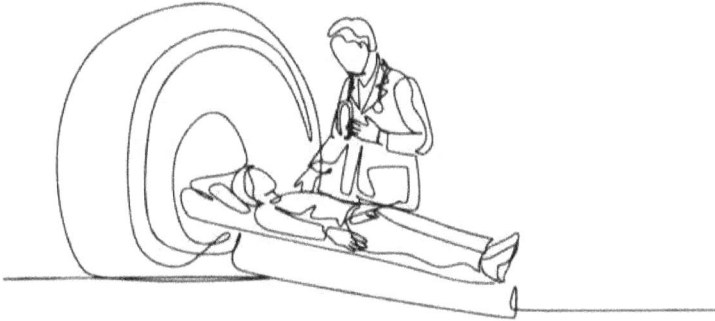

The first symptoms that the coronavirus is attacking the body include coughing, sneezing, and shortness of breath. The doctor is aware of these signs, but he cannot give a prescription until he knows if the virus has spread to the patient's lungs or not! Before he does anything else, he asks for a chest CT scan, which shows how far the virus has spread in the lungs. The scan helps the doctor figure out how the virus is acting in the lung, which makes it easier to treat the disease. Energy Scans make you a detective who has to find the places where your energy tank is leaking.

So, before we know how to use our energies well or badly, we need to learn about them in general. I use the idea of energy scanning to learn these things. An energy scan shows us where we lose energy and where we get energy. The scan helps us create a unique version of ourselves so that we can make better use of our energy.

In energy scanning, we look at daily events to see if they give us energy or take it away. By doing this, we learn that the events themselves are not important; instead, it is important whether they give or drain energy. By scanning the energies, we can find energy-drainers and either solve the problem in general or do something that takes less energy from us. Do you remember the time you did not want to hang out with your friends and said, "I'm okay; I just don't have the energy!" Why did you feel de-energised?

Energy detective

Do you know how energy expenditure occurs in the body's metabolism?

The immune system uses some of the calories we get from the food we eat. Calories are also used up by the digestive system. These calories are taken in without our knowledge or control. The same is true for our internal energy. Things happen in the deepest parts of your being, the unconscious, and these things are consuming your energy.

For example, childhood mechanisms, bad things that have happened to you, and many other things drain your energy without you realising it.

When you scan your energies, you can find out what parts of you are using energy without your awareness.

Like a detective, figure out the unconscious use of energy.

Energy Scan

Why does my energy go up and down? I worry about these fluctuations.

If you know what gives you energy and what drains it, you can easily control these changes.

There are two general rules for energy scanning. If you pay attention to them, you can do a better scan.

A) Monitor the amount of energy taken by each event.

How do you interpret each event?

What kind of energy does this interpretation give you?

You run into an old friend on the street after a long time. How do you feel about this? How much energy have you gained or lost in this event?

You open the door to your apartment, tired and hungry. When you open the door, you can smell your favourite food. You become so happy and full of energy that you forget your exhaustion.

Events reach our minds through our five senses, and we figure out what they mean based on our knowledge and beliefs. If we know what events give us energy or drain it away, we can figure out how each event fits into the energy equation.

Events are not important; their energy is.

Energy scanning helps us understand how each event affects us, and how we can use each event to our advantage.

b) Make your own energy scanner

Our emotions are directly affected by what we did when we were kids. People are taught in different ways, and the same way of teaching two people leads to different results. For example, the critical education method makes two children feel different things. For example, someone is hurt by criticism, someone works harder to make up for mistakes, others feel helpless and do not care about their work, and still, other people think others are not grateful because they always criticise and do not appreciate their work. Criticism helps one person do well, but it makes others feel bad about themselves and feel like they have failed. The way people work is affected by these different feelings that come from what they did as kids.

There are no fixed rules about how different people will feel about events. Every event is seen through the lens of a person's personality traits because everyone's subconscious mind is unique. Hence, the ultimate energy scan for each person is different. The only rule that is always true is that you should pay attention to your own energy and see what gives you energy and what drains it.

The rule: Everyone has a unique version of themselves.

Energy-drainers

Why do you feel like your energy is being sucked out of you and that your inner tank is empty? What consumes this energy? Where does your energy go?

Do you know how parasites live and behave? We know that a parasite is an organism that lives on or inside its host and gets the food it needs to survive from the host.

The energy-drainers act just like parasites. They eat very small amounts of food, and their life and survival depend on the energy they get from us. Because of this, they can be thought of as energy-drainers.

There are a lot of things in your life that drain your energy. Energy-drainers include all things that consume our energy.

I return to the Harry Potter movies again to help you understand what this term means. The name "Energy-drainer" makes me think of the dementors in the movie; wherever they were, there was hopelessness, sadness and death. When the dementors came, the air got cold and still. The wizards were attacked by bad thoughts, feelings, and memories, which drove them crazy and killed them. To get rid of the destructive power of the dementors, the wizards had to think about good things, good memories, and beautiful events in their lives. That was because the energy of these good memories could repel the energy of such faceless beings. Energy-drainers act like the dementors! In the "Energy Monster" section, examples of these "energy-drainers" are presented.

Some energy-drainers only use 1% or 2% of your energy, while others drain much more energy. However, altogether, they can all make us feel dispirited and disappointed or put an end to our efforts, because when the energy-drainers are at work, our desire and passions fade, and we feel empty. Some simple and common examples of energy-drainers are doubt, anxiety, lack of self-esteem, comparison, jealousy, anger, and many other things you can think of. Everybody has seen the destructive effects of these energy-drainers in their lives.

Don't be a blindfold horse

Energy-drainers steal the power of energy magicians to stop their spells from working. They are always making more and more of each other. This makes for an impaired cycle that seems impossible to break. Like an oil-extracting horse, people who are stuck in the cycle of energy-drainers cannot get out of this impaired cycle. The oiler covers the eyes of the horse to make it constantly rotate around the drilling machine. When the horse turns once, twice, or three times, it gets totally lost, forgets where it is, and has to keep turning for the rest of its life.

Let's avoid falling into the trap of energy-drainers by knowing them

A major energy-drainer called "The Blackhole"

You have probably heard about black holes in the news or in everyday life. The strangest and most amazing things in space show up after a supernova. Astronomy has shown that when big stars die, and their cores collapse, they leave behind black holes. Black holes are very dense, dark, and powerful, and their gravitational force is so strong that it beats all other forces. Not even light can beat gravity. Black holes swallow everything, and the more they swallow, the bigger and more powerful they become. Even scarier is that they cannot be seen or directly observed. The only way to tell what they are is by what is drawn toward them. Black holes are scary, dark, and huge masses that swallow everything.

Big energy-drainers do the same thing as small energy-drainers: they use up all or a lot of our internal energy. Thus, I call them "energy black holes".

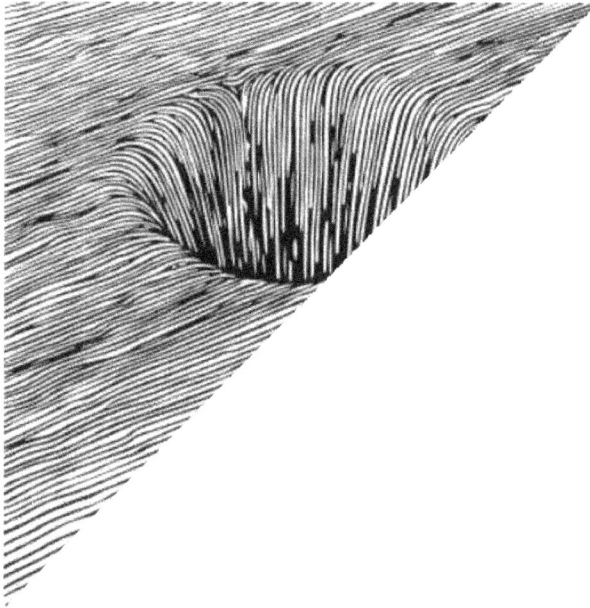

How can we tell if something that drains our energy is a black hole or an energy-drainer?

The answer is that the border between a black hole and an energy-drainer varies in different persons.

In my view, a black hole is anything that devours more than 50% of a person's energy.

In fact, you are dealing with a black hole if you are losing a lot of energy.

How are energy black holes made?

You might be surprised to learn that the energy black hole is created by you. You may be wondering how you can make them if you know nothing about it.

At first, the black hole is a small energy-drainer, but it gets bigger and hungrier as we feed it. The more energy we lose, the more energy is received by the energy-drainer, which turns it into a black hole that greedily drains up half or more of our energy.

Think about a couple who love each other but spend 50% to 80% of their energy on struggles and conflicts, draining them of their love. Undoubtedly, this relationship is a black hole. At first, it was a small energy-drainer, but they let it take all of their energy and grow into a powerful one that messes with their life and affects everything.

Similarly, someone who is in conflict with a colleague loses a lot of energy at work because their view of and relationship with that person have become a "black hole". They cannot keep their minds focused on their work, so they get bad results.

You may have seen Miyazaki's animated movie Spirited Away. In one part of this anime, an invisible creature with no face goes to a motel. In the beginning, it is not only not scary, but no one even notices it, and it starts to eat, and when it cannot find anything else to eat, it eats the people who live there until it grows into a big, scary monster that no one can escape from. When the main character takes him away from the motel, the monster loses its feeding source and slowly goes back to being the same quiet, harmless creature it was before.

Sometimes, our black holes used to be very simple and unimportant, but when they drained our energy and got stronger, they became very complicated and unsolvable. Often, if you stop them from using energy and do not feed them, they lose some of their complexity over time and become the same simple thing they were in the beginning.

When a small energy-drainer becomes a black hole, it uses up a lot of your energy.

Energy-drainers live with us, but they will be eliminated if we do not feed them for a while.

Black Hole Monster

In the first part of the story Demonata, by Darren

O'Shaughnessy, it is said that the boy had to play chess with an ugly, cruel monster. The monster was inimitable in chess. The boy would have to be killed if he lost, and he would also be killed if he did not want to compete. The boy was not very good at the game, so taking part in the competition would only put off his death. He did not want to die, though.

The monster and the boy sat on opposite sides of the big chess board at the table. The monster was sure that he was better than the boy, so he grinned, followed the boy's movements, and moved his chessmen freely. The boy was confused and upset, and he knew he had no chance against this chess genius. The monster got more energetic as the boy got more desperate. The boy had acquiesced to play to avoid dying, but if he kept going like this, the monster's claws would suffocate him for sure. He had to find a way! He had to take a leap in the dark in this game. He had to find a way different from the rules of the chess game to get rid of the disappointment and terminate the monster's happiness.

The boy realised that the sadder he felt, the more energetic the monster became. He realised that the monster was feeding on his sadness and gaining strength. The monster was sure to win and a trickle of drool leaked from the corner of its mouth. The boy told himself that he may not be able to beat him at chess, but he could do something that would make him lose. So, he did not care about defeating the monster in the game and turned it into a happy game for himself. He did not want to compete anymore; he just wanted to enjoy playing and have fun.

How do you think he gave himself the energy to overcome his fear, despair, and helplessness? What force was stronger than skill in the game?

When the boy decided to beat the monster, he thought about his family. He smiled when he thought about happy moments with his family. At that moment, his mother's scolding for breaking the window glass felt sweet, and his father's frown for not cleaning the garden and his sister's screams were all beautiful. The boy loved his family and thought about this love. He remembered whispering with his sister, as they wanted to surprise their mom on her birthday. He remembered the first time he raced a bike with his dad, and how he purposely fell down and lost. What a lovely day it was when he helped his mom make a birthday cake for his sister. He thought about the kisses from his parents, and as he remembered them, happiness flowed through him and turned into energy. He smiled at every memory he thought of, which made the monster even more confused. Love fed the boy with happiness. The boy was happy because he was loved. The monster was terrified by love. The monster was scared of being happy. The boy was no longer terrified of the chessmen thrown out of the screen by the monster.

What happened in your opinion? The monster's energy came from the boy's feelings of depression, sadness, and helplessness, but as time went on, the monster lost its energy sources. He could no longer just relax and be sure he would win. Even its chess skills became useless. The monster had lost control over everything. The monster could not continue the game, so it lost.

This monster is your black hole.

Energy flows to where there is interest. If you love what you do, you can do it over and over again, even after you fail. When you put love into your work, you get energy from it.

How can energy black holes be eliminated?

If you want to fight energy black holes, here are

some guidelines. You can find more ways and add them to this list.

A. Getting rid of the black hole by solving the problem

Sometimes, a small problem drains all your energy, and sometimes a big problem does the same. One way is to look at the problem from all sides and try to figure out how to fix it. Even things that seem simple can use up a lot of your energy, so you should focus on solving those things first to get the problem fixed as soon as possible.

B. Not feeding the black hole

Sometimes the problem cannot be fixed, or it takes a long time to fix. In such cases, you should be able to accept it and find a way to deal with it so that you do not waste your energy. Accepting that you cannot solve a problem shows that you are a mentally mature person. In this case, you can stop feeding the black hole and prevent it from getting bigger by not paying attention to it, finding a way to deal with the problem, or practicing how to live with it.

Black holes gradually weaken and become destroyed if they are unable to swallow energy.

C. The Seesaw technique

Sometimes, you have to deal with things that drain your energy, but what we have mentioned so far does not work. What can you do?

The answer is to use the "seesaw" technique. This is how you should get more energy. Coordinate energy gain with energy loss. For example, you could do a boring imposed job and your favourite job in parallel.

When there is an energy-drainer on one side that takes some of your energy, you should find an energy-giver and put it on the other side, so that you can keep your energy level from going down. Energy-givers are good ways to deal with people who take your energy. In the same way, when a black hole is taking up a lot of your energy, you need a "super-energiser" to make up for it, which will be discussed in the next chapter.

Let's use an example to make this clear

Imagine that someone has an accident while driving. Her eyebrow and nose are injured because of this accident. After recovering her health, she thinks she is not as pretty as she used to be, which makes her sad. When she thinks about this issue too much, she loses her self-confidence. She stops going to gatherings and feels more and more depressed.

Even though her face has not changed much, it has become an energy-drainer, and all the attention she pays to this issue has turned it into a black hole.

We said that one way to get rid of a black hole is to solve the problem. For example, the above person can get rid of the flaws she feels in her face by having a plastic or cosmetic surgery.

Yet, not everyone can always have these kinds of surgeries. Here, you can use the second method. In other words, this person can get happy with the way she looks now and know that her skills and values are not based on how pretty she looks. By accepting this problem, she can spend her time and energy on more important things and stop feeding the black hole.

Even if the second solution does work, she may still feel uncomfortable with her new face. Now, to make up for the energy she's losing, she needs to find energy-givers and super-energisers. Maybe learning something new or doing something she used to enjoy will give her the energy she needs to get through the day. Many pianists throughout history have turned to the piano to regain their energy when they were going through difficult times or suffering. These people became stars and sparkled in the centre of this energising shelter.

Most of the time, we cannot eliminate an energy black hole, but we can stop it from devouring our energy.

One thing is to destroy black holes, and another is to stop them from sucking up energy.

Threatening energy-drainers

We have already said that energy-drainers steal your energy like parasites and use it to grow bigger and bigger until they turn into black holes. Big energy-drainers endanger the energy magician since they easily turn into black holes. The energy magician's powers are also taken away by black holes. You can take better care of your energy magician if you know about such dangers.

We know that anything bad, like fear, low self-esteem, daily incidents, toxic relationships, and thousands of other things can drain our energy. However, there are some big energy-drainers that are not on the above list and might surprise you. Perfectionism is an example in that regard.

Let me tell you a story. I knew a young man who wanted to start making men's suits, but he never did anything about it. Instead, he just talked about his ideas and dreams. Once, when he started talking about his dreams again in a friendly group, I asked, "You've been talking about this for a while. Why haven't you done anything yet?" He said, "I want to make suits that are better than Hacoupian's and the best in the world. I won't settle for less than that."

I told him, "As long as you are saying these words, not only will you not have the best suit company in the world, but you also will not have even a small suit company." The young man felt much pain, but what I told him was true. In his dreams, he had made his products perfectly, but he was not able to do that in real life. His perfectionism made him helpless and afraid of failing.

Every great work begins with a very small point. The young man could have started his dream with a small local production and grown and improved it over time, but he did not because he thought he had to be the best from the beginning. Perfectionism had taken away his ability to take risks. To be honest, perfectionism always makes it hard to start. No matter how good your idea is, it is useless until you put it into action. "Two hundred words do not equal half an action[1]," says Saadi, the prominent Persian poet.

"Success" is the next big energy-drainer.

Success seems to be good, just like perfectionism, but it is one of the mose significant energy-drainers.

Success is an energy-drainer when it is the only goal and does not lead to something bigger. Success, as a final goal, is seen as a kind of stopping point for the mind, which makes it hard to move beyond and take the next big steps. We will talk more about this in the Success and Failure chapter.

Success and perfectionism make people afraid of failing, not being popular, not being as good as they usually are, not being the best, and comparing themselves to others or to their former selves. This makes it hard to take small steps and risks.

The next big energy-drainer is "comparing".

When you compare your life to other people's lives, especially celebrities' lives on the Internet, you make yourself unhappy with your life and lose a lot of energy. In this case, social networks, especially

---

[1] Actions speak louder than words

Instagram, act as an energy-drainer. The relationship between the level of life and energy has been discussed in the Ownership and Energy chapter.

Another example is "anxiety" and "self-humiliation".

When you are worried about doing something or stressed out about failing, you start to blame yourself, feel guilty, regretful, and helpless, and you always punish yourself with these feelings. You keep asking yourself why did I not use my opportunities and resources better. I should have done this. I wish I had made this or that choice. If I had gone in a different direction...!

It is enough to just get rid of these boring words. These "what-if's", "if-only's", and "why's" consume your energy in a terrible way and deplete any amounts of energy that may remain inside you.

Get rid of all these "what-ifs", "if-onlys", and "whys".

Sometimes, you justify your failures. If you always try to explain why you did what you did, you fall into the trap of an energy-drainer. If you cannot admit that you made a mistake, you cannot fix it. By defending yourself, you lose the chance to look at your work objectively and judge it.

With justification, we never recognize our mistakes.

The "sense of possession" is another energy-drainer.

This feeling makes you worry all the time that you might lose something you own. The culture of consumerism has prompted many people to spend their energy working hard from dusk to dawn throughout their lives to possess more things, raise their standard of living, and increase their welfare, and this has entrapped them in a cycle of "wasting energy for more possessions". People waste a lot of energy because they want to feel like they own something and take care of it. This takes so much energy that it keeps them from enjoying life. People with this trait always worry that they will lose or run out of what they have.

If you do not understand the concept of ownership well, it will take up all your time and energy. In the fifth chapter, this problem is discussed in more detail.

"Incomplete files" are among the biggest energy-drainers.

Look around you. Make a list of your unfinished tasks. How many tasks have you started but not finished? Unfinished tasks and open files drain your energy, just like open apps on a mobile device that drain the battery power. Tasks that are not finished waste your energy because they are always in the back of your mind as proof that you cannot finish things. When you finish tasks that you have not completed for a long while, your energy will go up.

Shut down your incomplete files.

"Illness" is another energy-drainer.

"A healthy mind lives in a healthy body," says an old proverb. Any kind of disease, big or small, can drain much energy, from something as simple as a toothache to something as complicated as cancer. This is true whether the disease is temporary and short-term or permanent and long-term. If we do not take good care of ourselves, we end up losing a lot of energy.

These are examples of big things that use a lot of energy and could easily turn into a black hole. If we can stop our energy from being sucked up from the beginning, these energy-drainers will stay the same or get weaker and smaller, but if they have already turned into a black hole, we need to balance our energy into something bigger than a simple energiser.

We need a super-energiser.

Are you unaware of super energisers? That's alright! In the next chapter, we will talk about a remarkable and redemptive super energiser: **Start!**

Chapter Three: Starting

Starting is the biggest step

Am I truly ready to start?

Find your path

Start taking steps

Obstacles to starting

Risk tolerance against stereotyping

Success happens by chance

Starting is an opportunity

Regrets

Dream Monday

Take a leap of faith and Start

Tiny steps

The top 5%

Simple, playful ideas to mind-blowing,
worldwide results

Have you ever not started working on something and then regretted it? Why do you think you did not start at that moment? What stopped you from doing it? Do you constantly prepare yourself for the perfect opportunity to start, or you have ventured and just started?

Starting is a fundamental and important energiser. The magic of energy is activated by starting, and it neutralises the power of energy-drainers. However, you might wonder "How can I start?"

Starting is the biggest step

Imagine a family planning to take a one-week trip during the summer. They keep planning to prepare for the best circumstances for the trip: "No one's sick, right? Are we taking enough clothes? How's the road? Are the roads we're taking too twisty? Which days have the least traffic? How's the weather? It's not going to rain, is it?' They probably find excuses for cancelling the trip, things as small as their young child's sneezing, and do not go on the trip this summer. Now, imagine the young children of that family. Their friends call them one day and ask if they are ready for the ride of their lives. In less than an hour, they have packed all their necessities in a backpack and are on the road.

Whether they hit traffic on the road, whether it is rainy or sunny, what does it matter? All that matters is that they are going on a friendly trip to have fun during the summer days.

Doing anything requires a start line so that the Energy Magician can cast his spells. If you fill the kettle but do not turn on the stove, the water will never boil, and you will never drink your tea! This is a simple example of starting and letting the energy flow. When something is started, the Energy Magician will always do his job. It does not matter how perfect your start line is; all that matters is taking action and moving forward.

Nevertheless, energy-drainers do not stay idle for long! When you want to start something, a thousand thoughts bombard your brain and make starting it harder than it already is, sometimes even impossible. For example, you do not have the skills and abilities to do something, you do not have enough knowledge or money, the competition is fierce, etc. You will also face naysayers and other obstacles right before starting something.

Are knowledge and skill ever enough? How necessary is money when prices are constantly fluctuating? All these are justifications we use to not start! That is exactly before starting, energy-drainers awaken and start fighting the Energy Magician. Energy-drainers use attractive and convenient reasons like "There'll be a better opportunity", "some other opportunities", and "Tomorrow's not going anywhere" to neutralise the magician's powers.

You must just start!

Before you read the rest of this page, ask yourself: Am I actually ready to start? Write down your answer right here on this page. You will ask yourself this question again at the end of the chapter. Then, you will have to compare your two answers and see if they are different. Your second answer is your new mind-set toward starting. This mind-set determines your energy and motivation levels for achieving things.

Start and get energised. Starting is the biggest energy-giver; it is a super-energiser. If you start walking down a certain path, no power can stop the starting of energy. Energy is the light and living stream, and it gives people the will to live and move forward. A young child is always moving forward. Anytime they do something, it is new for them;

repetition does not mean anything to children. While learning to speak, every time children say a new - albeit - incomplete, word, they get motivated to learn new words and speak more. Their never-ending starting energy propels them forward.

Starting is a powerful engine and a unique bargaining chip against fear and not-improving. Use it so you can fill yourself with energy and always have a winning hand. When something starts, it will move forward. The secret of life is just that simple: starting, getting energised, and moving forward on your path.

Set out on the journey toward your goals, starting with the super-energizer.

Starting with the primary push that fills you with energy. A powerful push that helps you soar. Just like an airplane engine that pushes the airplane off the ground and makes it soar into the sky.

When something gets started, fears and anxieties start fading and can be easily overcome. Therefore, starting is considered a super-energiser that fights against the black holes of energy. When you start doing something, the energy black holes stop being so terrifying, and worries are replaced with energy that fights the energy black holes.

Now that you know starting is a super-energiser, start doing something, no matter how small it is. How much energy do you have to move forward?

Never ever underestimate the starting energy potential.

What goals would be achieved if people just waited around and did not start anything? As the old Persian saying goes: "You can't just say candy and expect to taste it!" To climb a ladder, one must always start at the bottom and work their way up. Looking at the top step only increases the fear of climbing and ensures that the ladder is never climbed. We must not give in to these fears; all the ladders in the world are the same; you just need to take the first step.

Never wait for an invitation, help, or the perfect conditions to take the first step in anything. Taking the first step will create favourable conditions for you.

To cross the dangerous path toward Leili's

The first requirement is to be Majnoon

(Leili and Majnoon by Hafez, a Persian poem about two lovers)

We wanted and were ready to produce a pitch but had not received an operation license yet. We had to go through a long and excruciating process to obtain the license. Did the lack of a license that we would soon receive stop us? We began production. The Ministry of Industry, Mine, and Trade informed us that we could not sell the products before the license was issued and could only try pilot production. When they saw our determination and capabilities in production, they facilitated the procedures for receiving the license and issued the document in much less time.

To be honest, we were not completely informed of the regulations when we started to work and entered the operational phase. However, we started because the energy released by starting is powerful enough to face any issues.

When you have a business idea, you cannot predict the future obstacles and challenges with certainty until you actually start working. Others can share their experiences with you regarding some obstacles, but the vision illustrated by those experiences absolutely depends on whether the person failed or succeeded. Because the vision is created by someone else, you are constantly wondering how to prepare for the job. What tools will I need? What if I face the same problems, as well? What should I do to prevent them? There is a missing link in this vision! You are not analysing the real situation. Rather, you are reviewing the experiences of others and using them to predict your own future. You are the missing link from this perspective. As long as you do not start something, no experiences or information can predict your future in that field.

You should use the experiences of others to gain a preliminary understanding of your chosen field. These experiences are not guidelines for how to do something. They are just information about different aspects of the job.

Everyone has a unique way of achieving experiences and results. If someone fails at something, it does not mean you will fail at it, as well. Doing anything means a new start on a new path. Tree leaves fall during autumn, and we only see beautiful and colourful leaves on the ground, but every single leaf falls in a certain way. Look at how they spin down to the ground. They spin towards the ground in different ways. Every snowflake has a special shape; in other words, no two snowflakes look completely the same. Consider your fingers; your fingerprints are different from those of all the humans who have ever lived; they are unique. So is everyone's DNA. If you were familiar with the structure of atoms, you would know that electrons' quantum numbers are unique to them. There are thousands of examples like this in the world, and they all indicate that the universe is constantly taking different shapes and changing. The entire universe experiences a new beginning every single moment.

Despite their similar experiences and shapes in the past, new beginnings always open new doors to new fields.

Many people have climbed Mount Everest. Many of them never reached the summit, but that does not mean the next person cannot achieve the goal. The next person might do it in record time. If someone reaches the summit once, that does not mean they can do it again next year. Or if somebody did not reach the summit, who says they cannot reach it the next time they try? Many factors affect our results; in this scenario, they include physical and psychological conditions, tools and equipment, weather conditions, etc. Nonetheless, every time someone decides to climb Mount Everest, they are stepping on a new path; because doing anything means a new start on a new path. In this scenario, everybody climbs the same mountain, hoping to reach the same summit, but no two climbers go through identical journeys.

Starting means being the first. No matter how many times other people have attempted something, it is completely new when you start it because no two people go through the same journey. People cannot repeat old experiences, because life is creative by its nature.

When two people have different personalities and characteristics, their conditions and experiences will never be the same. Therefore, they will have different priorities for starting and doing something.

The experiences of others come from their courses that might be similar to yours, but they are most definitely not yours.

Find your course

Every day is different from the previous ones. Every day is a new and unique experience. Even daily tasks and routines do not happen the same way twice. Even if they happen in the same spot and time, there will always be at least one different aspect.

In the movie "Groundhog Day", the protagonist is trapped on a certain day of his life, February 2nd. That day keeps repeating events that appear to be identical. Every time the clock reaches midnight, February 2nd starts again. However, even through all of this, every day, there is one thing different; the protagonist. Without even knowing it, the protagonist goes through his repetitive day in a different manner. He is a new person every day.

The reality is that you turn into a different person every day. Compare your mood with how it was yesterday; you are not similar to the person you were yesterday. When you are a different person every day, your courses are different from others, as well. In this case, how can two people go through the exact course toward success?

Starting puts you on your personal and unique path, and the Energy Magician uses his abilities and powers to help you discover it.

Start taking steps

Stepping on a new course means facing obstacles

that require creative and novel solutions. Your course will not be like anyone else's; you must just start and move forward. Starting can provide us with an accurate understanding of the journey. Oftentimes, the only way to understand the characteristics of a job is by starting, failing, and starting again, smiling at small successes, and most importantly, comparing results to actions. That means asking yourself: "What did I do to get these results? What can I do to improve them?" When you start something, a new path toward your goals gets shaped.

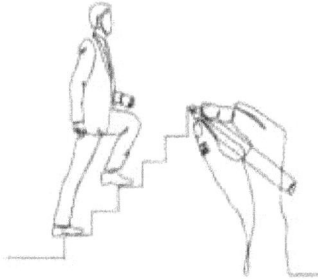

Factors that prevent starting

"Clean your room", "How lazy you are! You still haven't watered the flowers!", "How hard is it to walk down the street and buy milk?" Thousands of similar sentences can be mentioned here, as everybody has heard them from their family members or friends (or has told them such sentences).

Procrastinating doing something we have done before is called "being lazy." It can be for anything; watering a flower, or even re-doing an old project. When we do not have the energy and willpower required to do something, the desire to stay in the safe and comfortable zone is an energy-drainer that blocks the starting super-energiser. The "remain safe and still" energy-drainer is very seductive. Breaking out of the safety zone requires a great amount of energy. However, the second you get up and start, the super-energiser is activated, and you will not need to put in so much energy anymore because things are already in motion. When a new and unknown journey that has not been experienced before is ahead, the biggest obstacles to starting are fear and the desire to maintain the current conditions (Inertia). Newton's first law is about Inertia: objects wish to maintain their current conditions. When you do not want to leave the bed in the morning, you wish to maintain your current condition. Here, the Inertia law prevents movement and starting. How do we overcome this law? It is simple. Make a start!

When we want to move an object, most of our energy goes into moving it from the starting position. We are putting all our energy into overcoming the Inertia of stillness. Whenever you feel like remaining still, remind yourself that "Inertia is keeping me still," and use all your willpower and energy right then. When you start moving, you will not need so much energy to keep yourself in motion.

You must have friends who keep to themselves during every ceremony and stay motionless. In every celebration and ceremony, you probably insist that they get up just for a little bit and dance, though they constantly refuse to do so.

You constantly insist, and they refuse until, at one point, they get up and keep dancing so much that you start begging them to sit down before making a scene.

According to Newton's first law, your friend was in a state of stillness, your insistence had the energy to put them in motion, and now they could not be stopped.

The energy released by starting is usually enough to see that task through. Many tasks are completed solely with the starting energy.

The fear of doing something causes anxiety about the unknown and failure. If you prefer to stay in your comfort zone, avoid starting new projects as much as possible. Then, you will never have to face the unknown.

Unknown fields mean you do not know the preparations, basic elements, tools and equipment you might need in that field.

Starting means entering new worlds you do not know anything about, and even if past experiences give you some information, it does not mean things are going to be like that this time.

Making a start comes with taking risks.

Risk tolerance against stereotyping[2]

There's a commonly used Persian expression: "You may know by a handful the whole sack." This expression is about stereotyping, because it sees everything from one perspective. Imagine going to a city for the first time and visiting a grocery store

---

[2] A very simplified view of reality is called stereotyping. This type of thinking is most attractive to people who judge others by their values and label people who are different from themselves. This method prevents logical judgment toward others and causes people to judge others based on little information and the thinker's cliché imagination, which are based on society and social media, as well.

for a specific product. The store staff rudely inform you that they do not have that product and yell at you to leave if you are not going to buy anything.

You would leave the store, hurt and angry, and consider that rude person a representative of that city and judging all its citizens based on that one interaction. This judgment is caused by stereotyping. This type of thinking prevents rational judgments about others. In this attitude, the characteristics of one person are generalised to an entire society. This type of thinking is hard to change. An example is the improper jokes people make about other cities and ethnicities. Stereotyping is caused by the brain's comfort-seeking nature when confronted with massive amounts of data from the environment. Stereotyping consumes energy and trains the brain to become accustomed to not thinking and laziness. Our brain creates stereotyping to simplify matters. Stereotyping informs us about the preparations, tools, and equipment we are going to need in certain situations. It assures our safety and preserves our comfort zones. College lessons are great examples of stereotyping. Most college students get great grades in college but fail in their jobs and businesses. That is not surprising since they were successful in a dead science, a studied and proven science in which every aspect had been determined before. Such sciences are not secrets to be discovered, but the business world is a living and unknown science. It is very unpredictable. Business success requires us to tolerate risks and face the unknown. Risk tolerance puts people in jeopardy. When you are in jeopardy, you do not have a long-term plan, and that is worrying. Jeopardy requires us to think. You must analyse every step you take and its results, improve them, and know the path ahead of you at the same time. We are not used to thinking; an Islamic saying says, "One hour of thinking is more valuable than 70 years of praying." We might not think for an hour in our whole lives. Thinking is an open space free of assumptions. Thinking means looking at issues independently to challenge them. Thinking gives us new insights into our issues and problems.

When Hafez says: "Dark nights, fear of waves, and terrifying whirlpools/What do we carefree people on the shores know of such things," I believe he is referring to comfort zones. The people resting on their safe shores will never understand life's troubles.

I will tell you the experience of a young doctor and his patient, so you can understand the importance of risk tolerance better. A sick man, who had been turned down by many specialist doctors, hopelessly asked a young doctor to treat him. The man's body was covered with pus-filled boils, which destroyed his nervous system and lowered his cognitive abilities as they got deeper and would, finally, result in a very painful death.

The young doctor wondered what the treatment was, and why the other experienced doctors refused to perform it. It turned out that the doctors could get infected with the disease if the operation was not correctly performed. The young doctor had not had any similar experiences and did not know whether he could handle it. Moreover, if he touched the patient's skin, he would get infected, as well. The young doctor told the patient about the hard and painful treatment method, said he had not experienced such an operation before, and that there was a fifty percent chance he might fail. He also told him that the disease would painfully kill him one day. The patient had to decide whether to let the inexperienced doctor perform the painful operation or accept his painful fate. The doctor and the patient accepted the risks of what they were going to do anxiously and painfully. At first, the young doctor was scared. However, the further he moved, the more confidence he found in himself, the more he understood the intricacies of the operation, and the more determined he got to save his patient. The operation was performed. Afterward, the patient woke up and saw his bandaged body. He realised he had been saved and given a new chance. Taking risks might cause a lot of anxiety, but it also energises you to try and do better.

Success is accidental

Most self-help books and even educational systems constantly repeat that "success is not a chance." You must have encountered things like "Success only depends on you", but I do not believe in them. I certainly believe in chance and believe many successes happen by chance. We have all had our lucky days and reached things by accident at least once. The only important point is to expose yourself to these accidents by starting.

You have probably heard the saying "take a chance while it is available; successful people are those who take it." I believe that you can get many chances; all that matters is taking risks and opening the door for them.

Let's take a look at chance from a statistical point of view:

Imagine you have started working on something. You have a 50 percent chance of success or failure. If you succeed and get the desired results, you will move on to a new stage. But imagine you have failed. If you start again and take the risk of a second failure, you have moved on to a new phase. There is a 25 percent chance of failing both attempts. Therefore, the possibility of failure decreases.

Now, imagine your second attempt fails, as well. But you are so determined you try again, and this time, there is only a 12.5 percent chance of failure.

If you are willing to get to this point and start again after every failure, your chance of failure gets smaller and smaller, while your chance of success gets bigger every time.

A simple calculation can show how important taking risks and starting is.

Starting is an opportunity

Starting and stepping on a new journey is a unique aspect of using the opportunity of life. New challenges in life provide you with opportunities for new actions. Exploiting these opportunities in a timely manner can give you enough energy to finish your journeys.

The loss of unique opportunities is behind most of our regrets and disappointments. Opportunities can appear in a split second and then vanish. You must seize all the opportunities life presents to you. Recognising opportunities allows the Energy Magician to release his magic. You can never know what opportunities life will present you with next. Humans cannot control events and opportunities, but we can give meaning to them because everybody gets unique opportunities of their own. When you use the experiences of others as your only guide, you will lose the unique and golden opportunities on your path, and you will keep postponing your starts because your opportunities are not in their experiences, and you cannot find them that way. Successful people do not see existence as something fixed and monotonous; they take responsibility for every event on their journeys and transform them into energisers. Energetic people see their entire journey as an opportunity to find new opportunities and new starts. They believe that every moment of life is rich and new. Successful people were not necessarily given more or better opportunities. Everyone gets many opportunities, but successful people are the ones who start sooner. Unsuccessful people keep denying the richness of life. For them, everything is already clear and determined, and there is nothing new to experience. In their perspective, the novelty of opportunities is meaningless.

Oftentimes, starting late means all the opportunities are gone, and there is nothing to achieve anymore.

Many times, I have taken certain initiatives that our competitors were considering, as well. Every time, I started working on them without wasting any time, and before anyone else did, I became a pioneer in that field and achieved the best results. By the time my competitors started, the market had already been saturated.

You might be wondering, "how can I recognise such opportunities?"

To recognise opportunities, you must improve your understanding of them and learn the skills needed to recognise them.

But how can you do that?

It is simple. Always imagine that there are unique opportunities in front of you. Look at every moment of life as a new opportunity for a new start, take risks and step onto new journeys so you can get energised, and recognise golden opportunities. Fearing new starts and waiting means losing invaluable opportunities. What opportunities are there in your life right now? What new opportunity were you presented with today? Which one of them have you recognised but not yet had the time to take the initiative on them? Is it still accessible to you?

Let's talk about a ground-breaking start-up company in the transportation field. You have surely heard of the brand "Uber." The online taxi app automatically connects passengers to the nearest drivers. Uber even managed to become the highest-valued start-up company in the world.

The story of this company starts with two American friends on a trip to Europe. After failing to find a taxi at midnight to take them to their hotel in Paris, they hired a private driver for 800 dollars. They decided to find a way to lower their transportation costs. That decision led to what we now know as Uber.

From the beginning, Uber's innovation put it on the radar of many investors and it is now active in 66 countries. However, the founders of Uber did not have an easy time with it. They faced numerous threats of all kinds from the taxi industry and taxi drivers who considered their jobs in danger. Uber had to fight competitors and American politicians to get to its present position. They are still fighting for the right to use self-driving cars.

Thousands of people had faced the same problem before those two friends, needing a taxi and not finding one. They might have even had similar ideas, but none of them took any initiative.

You might remember a time when you needed to call the nearest taxi agency to get a ride. Sometimes, you could not find its phone number. Sometimes, finding a 24/7 agency was difficult. Some other times, all their drivers were busy, and it would take at least an hour for one to become available. People would usually find a different transportation method, and if that was not possible, they would wait for the taxi and waste a lot of time.

When the *Snapp!* start-up company created a domestic version of Uber, many of the people employed in the taxi industry considered it a threat to their careers. They could not adapt to such a massive change and slowly lost their jobs. However, many saw this change as a new opportunity. An opportunity for new jobs. They identified new business opportunities, learned new skills, and used them to improve themselves and their careers.

The Coronavirus pandemic is a similar situation in which people's careers and lives face a massive challenge. Great losses and global sympathy were felt across the world. Many people felt anxious and threatened by the virus and the restrictions it caused, and considered normal opportunities to be lost. They did nothing but feel sad, and the loss of their loved ones caused them to lose even more opportunities. But is it not the case that life keeps going no matter what? Is it not better if we face and overcome difficulties and move on? While facing the difficulties of the pandemic and the losses caused by it, some people adapted to the situation and tried to improve their lives, create new job opportunities, and turn the world into a better place.

A friend of mine and his family used all the extra free time they had during the pandemic to help people and produce homemade protective masks. As time went on and the demand increased, he bought a machine to produce masks in large numbers. At the same time, millions of people were experiencing depression due to the quarantine and the idleness caused by it. Mask production changed the course of his career, and he now owns a huge medical equipment production facility.

Did anyone have any experience in dealing with such a disease before the pandemic started? The pandemic was a new and unknown experience, and humans had no way to deal with it other than facing it head-on.

Find an opportunity in every situation.

The regret of not making a start

You should think about your past and identify all the opportunities you were presented with. Why are you shaking your head and feeling regretful? Oftentimes, regretting your inaction in the past takes much more energy than what is required to do something. Regret of not starting becomes an energy-drainer and creates a black hole. For example, people who want to go on a diet and start exercising, but do not actualise their plans, are constantly spending energy feeling regretful and sad about all the weight they have gained. If they had actually exercised, they would not have lost so much energy. They have turned their regrets into powerful energy-drainers. To prevent the creation of new energy-drainers, all you need to do is start working, and your energy will be released.

The Dream Monday

It is never too late to take new initiatives, and you should never lose the first chance you have at starting something. You can never know when you will have another opportunity like that again. If you have perfectly prepared everything for taking the initiative, I can assure you that you have started way too late. You have sacrificed many golden opportunities to get to this level of preparation. Ambitious and risk-tolerant people are great at taking the initiative and starting things; they welcome new days and challenges with open arms. Most people have the skills and abilities necessary to get their desired results, but they get the same results unskilled people get because they never take any initiative. I never wait for Monday to start something. My past experiences have taught me just how dangerous Dream Mondays can be. It can take away our motivation and make us forget about our goals entirely. To escape this trap, I use a very efficient method called "The Cycle of Progress." A cycle that neutralises the dream of a future Monday. In this cycle, every action has three steps.

The first and most important step is making a start.

Unless the first step is taken quickly and energetically, no successful results will ever be achieved in the world.

The second step is consistency and continuous improvement.

The key to the efficiency of the cycle is continuous improvement. Continuous improvement is the key to continuously increasing quality. Continuous improvement in things can overcome the dream of a perfect Monday because you are constantly reviewing and improving what you have started; you are constantly trying and planning; you are analysing your results and actions and trying to perfect them. Continuous improvement is a cycle of continuous starts and improvements, that raises the quality of what you are doing and gets you closer to the final step, achieving the goal.

Achieving the goal is the third step.

Achieving the goal does not mean ending your improvement cycle. It just means you have achieved a goal you set for yourself, and now it is time for a new one. The cycle of starting, continuous improvement, and achieving the goal applies to the new goal, as well. The improvement cycle saves you from the Dream Monday trap.

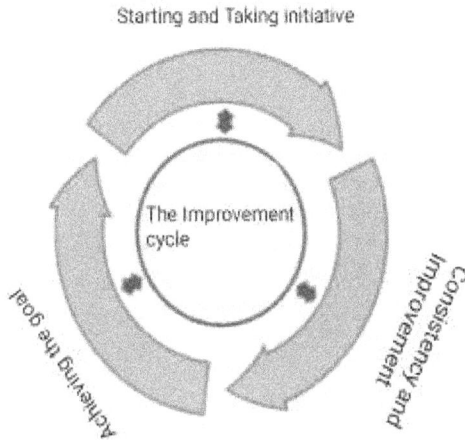

Starting and Taking initiative

The Improvement cycle

Achieving the goal

Consistency and Improvement

Go into the cycle of progress right now. Analyse one of your incomplete tasks according to the Improvement Cycle. In which step did you fail?

Most unsuccessful people are very weak at starting and taking the initiative. Do you think the "I'll start on Monday" mind-set can get you anywhere?

Waiting for certain situations or people is an excuse; you will never start anything with this mind-set. Some people do not start anything because they think they lack the required knowledge and skills, and they will certainly fail! Failure is possible even if you have all the equipment and expertise necessary, because something unexpected can happen at any moment that needs a new level of knowledge.

You do not need to be perfect to making a start, but you do need to start to become perfect.

So, make a start even if it is not a good and successful start.

The main reason behind procrastination is the fear of inability and failure. Most people are scared of taking the first step and keeping their Energy Magician in chains. Do you want to become a powerful starter? Then, believe that starting is a super-energiser.

No matter what you want to do, you must always make a start.

As long as you do not start, you will never be successful.

If you are scared of starting, it means you have already accepted failure. So, if you are going to fail, at least start so that you may fail at something useful. Apply the Improvement Cycle to your failures to learn from and overcome them. When you start, you are placed on the second step: Consistency and Improvement or actions and continuous adjustments.

Risk takers consider starting to be an amazing super-energiser. This super-energiser overcomes comfort zones and the Dream Monday and paves the way toward improvement and growth. Analysing the experiences of others and waiting for the perfect situation to start are just excuses for avoiding risks and do not help you start anything. Many people have been gathering information and planning a perfect start for a long time and have not started yet! On the other hand, some people immediately start working on their goals and pave their way using the continuous improvement mind-set. When you notice yourself putting off starting something, be aware that you are not on the continuous improvement cycle.

Venture and make a start!

Why taking the first step is so terrifying? Uncertainty about the results is the main cause of it. The rule that protects the brain says: "If you're not sure you will get your desired results, it is better not to do it." This rule is a trap and an energy-drainer.

How can we escape the trap of energy-drainers? Making a start is the point in which the course is found, and if we accept the fact that good and bad days are part of any journey, and failure is an inevitable part of the process, we would not be scared to start on new paths. If you believe that you are absolutely prepared for your journey and will not fail, I assure you that there is a great failure awaiting you. If you start by listening to your heart and taking a leap of faith, you can fight the not-starting energy-drainer. Which energy black hole can stand against a "leap of faith"? Starting with a leap of faith is a magic tool that throws you onto your path. Most people use the most common and well-known method when they want to start something. In that method, they consider every aspect before starting, consult the best experts in that field, and create the best team. They secure the required funds and prepare everything for their new journey. The biggest advantage of this method is its low chances of failure. Nevertheless, those who use it will eventually realise that they, like most others, did not achieve anything significant. At best, their results were similar to the results of others. This method is not innovative or creative. No new paths are discovered; therefore, no new results are achieved. It means doing the same things others have done before. The widespread "How to succeed" programs recommend this classic method, but I have chosen the "leap of faith" method to conquer the unknown and release my start energy. In this method, you must take a leap of faith and throw yourself into your new journey without wasting any time and face its challenges as they come. Taking a leap of faith is something we have all experienced at least once, and we know how much energy it gives us to finish our journey. You have probably decided to go on a trip with your friends without any previous planning many times. You probably did not even have enough money, but your heads were filled with dreams, so everyone put all their money together and had fun for a few days. Teenagers do things like this quite often because they are filled with passion and are not afraid of risks or taking new initiatives. Starting with a leap of faith means starting something without preparations or plans and thinking of those when you are already on the journey. That way, you will welcome new opportunities, gain new experiences, make decisions, and take action based on the situations you are facing.

People who take leaps of faith are rather pragmatist. Instead of obsessive planning, they move forward with energy and do what they believe is the right thing in every situation. In this method, you might not have all the requirements of the journey at the beginning, but your results and innovations will certainly be unique to you. You cross your path in a way that nobody else can. This method is a little scary, right? However, if you consider life carefully, you will realise that there is nothing more terrifying than losing opportunities, delaying, and not taking initiative.

When we launched our company's production line, we still had not built any walls around the plant because we could not afford it. We built the walls of our company when we were already operational and producing. However, most people would want to finish the infrastructure and the buildings first and start working in a perfectly designed and completed building with the most beautiful environment. Our organisation started working with small and limited storage units, but the only important thing was that we started.

In my opinion, "start quickly" and "acting pragmatically" in situations where not everything is ready are among the key secrets to success.

Starting everything with a leap of faith turns you into a creative person who is ready to face any challenge. I genuinely believe one of the reasons behind our current success is not relying on the experiences of others. The experiences of others can be useful, but they can also be energy-drainers that make sure people never start on their goals. In our modern world, you cannot go through any journey unless you do it by yourself. All you need to do is to reclaim your energy and stay consistent.

If you fall a hundred times, get up for the one hundred and first time and continue.

Statistics indicate that the majority of people believe the energy required for doing something must come from ourselves. However, I believe that as long as you immediately take action, your quick and powerful start will fill you with enough energy to finish the journey. In a 100-meter sprint race, what sets the winners apart from the others is their starting point. You must immediately start running with all your power. Do not worry about external obstacles; you will automatically get filled with enough energy to overcome them.

A friend of mine once asked me if I ever had a daughter, would I let her work for another company? I thought about that for a few minutes and then remembered something. When I was thirteen, my uncle had an advertisement company, and a few people worked there as typists. I was not one of their employees and did not get paid anything. However, I would sit in the office for hours after the typists had left and keep typing. In the beginning, I was so bad at it that the employees wanted me to stop because it took them a long time to correct my mistakes than it would have if they had typed the page themselves. I did not listen to them and kept working. After some time, I had gotten so good at it that I did not have to look at the monitor or the keyboard; I just stared at the page I was reading from. I never received any money for all that work, but I did learn a very useful skill at a very young age. So, if my future daughter ever wanted to work for an organisation other than my own, I would be very happy for her, because she would be starting something and gaining valuable experiences. At the core of everything, it is the small steps that provide you with the energy for bigger goals. Professional typing and managing an oil refinery are similar jobs at their cores, and small steps like learning to type provide the energy for bigger leaps like managing an oil refinery. The continuous improvement mind-set recommends that we learn life lessons from our own life experiences, not from what we hear from others. That is because others have learned their lessons from experiences that happened a long time ago, and following them gets you results that are not unique to you but similar to theirs. It does not matter what goals you choose for yourself, whether you want to get promoted or start your own company; your goals and destinations do not matter. The only thing that matters is taking the initiative and using the starting super-energiser.

That is the method I chose for myself. Along the way, I had many goals and worked in many industries, and all the lessons I learned from them resulted in the foundation of my refinery. I would have never thought that learning to type professionally would get me here someday, but that seemingly simple action provided me with the energy to get here. Whenever people learn from the challenges they face rather than the people they meet, they will succeed. I said all of these things to prove this:

Starting is one of the biggest super-energizers in the whole universe.

Tiny steps

Today, I am the CEO and founder of a refinery. That is quite a big achievement. You have no idea how many challenges I have faced along the way, and what lessons I have learned from them. You have no idea how many small steps and actions have resulted in this great achievement. It all started when my friend and I rented a room in a small office and started our work. Our goal was to import polymers. We had no knowledge about that job, and we had even gotten the idea from someone else. Our business plan was vague and imprecise. We never cared about why we had chosen such a goal.

Why we started that job did not matter.

All that mattered was that we had started doing something. In the end, we failed but learned so many new things that our path got shaped. We began as importers, grew remarkably, faced so many challenges, and learned so many things that we eventually became exporters.

When you start on a new journey, the journey itself leads you. Our journey led us to experience so many unexpected things such as producing and exporting pitch – among other things - because we believed that "The journey shall be your guide". Nowadays, I wholeheartedly believe that you should choose a goal for yourself, even if you are unprepared and in a bad situation, and start working toward it consistently; if you fall, you should get up and try again. Rest assured, your results will be much better than uselessly waiting around. When I was thirteen years old, I dreamed of learning to type professionally from my uncle's employees, and I took the initiative toward that dream. Even though typing is not really important to my current job, the experiences I gained along the way shaped my life for the better. For example, because I had learned to use my fingers quickly and accurately at a young age, I managed to learn how to play the piano very quickly and become a fairly good pianist. If you want to be led toward success, have the power to finish whatever you start. When I say, "have the power to finish whatever you start," I mean to have the power to fail and quickly get back on your feet, learn from your failure, and get enough energy from it for the rest of your journey. Failure is the best and newest experience you can gain in life. Achieving a goal means not giving up on it; it means getting back to work after every single failure until your goal has been achieved. You might be wondering, "What about our interests?" I am not denying the importance of interests, but who knows what they are interested in at the beginning? If you spend a long time trying to find something you are interested in, you are just wasting precious time. Start working on your goals, even if you are not interested in them. Your interests will present themselves to you on new journeys. In my experience, when people forgo unnecessary preparations and start working on something, they will develop an interest in it over time. That is because interest is just our mental occupation with the path we are on, and it is meant to overcome procrastination and delays. Choose your best idea and start working on it; you can never know what you will face along the way, but as long as you use the continuous improvement mind-set, you will develop an interest in it, or you will find your real interests and better ideas along the way. I recommend you start working on something and discover your interests through that.

Interests are discovered through new experiences.

It does not matter what you start; all that matters is that you start doing something.

The members of the 5% group

A Persian proverb says: "The fish is fresh no matter when you catch it." It means it is never too late to start. However, what should you start on? Which idea is good enough to start working on? While searching for an idea, be aware of mental traps such as, "I don't think this idea is good enough," "Others are already doing it," and "Too many people have had this idea for me to succeed at it."

If you have an idea, your unconscious mind probably considers it a suitable on for you; pay

attention to the messages of your unconscious mind.

In any business, only the top 5 percent are considered to be the most successful. They make the most money and are the first to take advantage of new opportunities; the other 95 percent are not satisfied with their results. Considering this, it does not matter what field you choose, you must join its top 5 percent to be successful. Therefore, you cannot label an idea as good or bad! The important thing is starting to work on it and achieving your goal. When you start working on an idea, there are two possible outcomes: you will either join the top 5 percent of people in that field, or you will join the average 95 percent. So, if you have an idea, just start working on it. What other people think about your idea does not matter. Rest assured, no matter what goal you choose, many people have failed at it before you. Their failures are not your path. You can only join that field's top 5 percent by learning from your failures and getting energized by small actions. Instead of spending all your life wondering what field would give you the highest chances of success, just start working on one. After failing a few times and getting back up on your feet, you will find the field most suited to you. Start working on something with all your power, and that will help you eventually find your true goal. This is exactly what I experienced in life, and the results have been amazing.

From simple and playful ideas to mind-blowing global results

Do you think Mark Zuckerberg knew what he was going to achieve when he founded Facebook? How precise was his business plan before he started? Did Zuckerberg have any idea that Facebook would lead to apps as popular as WhatsApp and Instagram? He certainly did not know any of that before starting on his idea. He was just a normal college student who had a simple and playful idea and started working on it with his friends. Along the way, they failed, got back up, and kept working consistently until they reached their current success. He most certainly did not expect his idea to go global at the beginning. He could not have imagined that his idea would later affect the outcome of the United States presidential election and earn him the title of the most influential man of the year. He had just started working on a simple website. After taking the initiative and working on it, his journey was shaped according to the public demands and expectations from Social Media platforms. After achieving his goals for Facebook, he set out to achieve new ones. Goals that led him to WhatsApp. Do you think he never failed along his journey? Do you believe he was not summoned to court many times? Do you think people did not tell him that his idea was useless, and that he was wasting his time? Do you believe people did not ask him if he was not tired of going to courts and answering questions over and over again? He faced all of these energy-drainers along the way.

If Facebook had not lost its popularity, and Zuckerberg had not experienced a decline in his success, he would have never bought and perfected Instagram at such an astronomical price. Instagram's success is not due to the success of Facebook; it was born from Facebook's saddest and worst days. Zuckerberg, just like every other successful person, learned that to achieve great success, you must start before everyone else, fail repeatedly, and start again.

Google was also a simple and playful idea dreamed up by two friends in a college dormitory. Everyone considered their idea to be laughable, but the friends did not pay them any heed. They worked on their idea, and eventually reached their goal. When asked if they had imagined their idea would one day turn into such a huge company, Google's co-founders said no. They said they never imagined reaching these results; they just wanted to connect two computers through a network and share some data. Google started as a vague and imprecise idea, but it was an idea that they could work on. They did; they started working on it with everything they had, they were consistent, faced their failures, and moved on from them until they reached their goals. Lack of preparations and bad conditions did not mean anything to them. Since their idea was so novel, no one could help them face the challenges on their journey because nobody had ever experienced them before. They learned to find a new path from deep inside the very challenge they were facing. So, every time Google failed, they got back up and kept moving forward until Google became what we know today. Their experience proves that the starting super-energiser can change the course of human history.

"DigiKala" is another example of a successful and modern business. Do you think DigiKala started just as it is today? Do you think it could offer the same services it did today when it started working? Again the answer is No.

DigiKala is the story of two Persian brothers who enthusiastically bought a camera from a foreign digital store but realised that it was a counterfeit. They could not return it and wondered why there was not anywhere where you could return counterfeit products. That is how DigiKala's idea was born; it was simple, vague, and imprecise. These two brothers were not computer programmers at the beginning, and they did not own huge storage facilities and equipment either. The internet infrastructure back then was not even suitable for an online business. However, the brothers started working on their idea, faced many challenges, failed repeatedly, and got back up. They gained valuable experiences along their journey and created DigiKala.

Take your small and simple ideas very seriously. They are the Energy Magician's playful tricks to get you moving. These small ideas can fill you with energy and lead to great results. Starting with a leap of faith should be your priority. When you start moving down a certain path, hitting obstacles is inevitable. These obstacles require you to find solutions that will help shape your true goals and bring you great success. Let's reverse-engineer DigiKala. Imagine if those two brothers aimed to reach their current position from the first day. Did they have the necessary knowledge and skills? How much knowledge and how many skills did it take for them to succeed? It is obvious that it took a great amount of knowledge and skill for DigiKala to reach its current condition. They needed to learn Computer Programming knowledge, tax regulations, human resources issues, etc. Let's say they could solve them by hiring an expert for each field. How were they going to survive market value challenges and investment issues? How were they supposed to dominate their target market and many other challenges we do not know about? If they had waited for the perfect conditions and perfect preparations, DigiKala would not be the main online market right now. If they had not started working on their idea immediately, they would still be preparing and learning, and others would have stolen this opportunity.

You might be thinking that "not knowing the path" is one of your shortcomings; I am here to tell you that it is one of your advantages. If you accept your lack of knowledge, you can learn a thousand different things in your journey and extract opportunities from challenges. If you believe that you know everything, you will provide a prepared answer to every question and obstacle and never take the time to think, learn, and innovate. Not knowing makes you think, and thinking provides you with numerous different creative solutions.

When DigiKala was founded, many people with bigger funds and more knowledge competed with the brothers, but they all failed. Why do you think this happened? I would say that the arrogance of knowledge caused them to start later. Nowadays, you can create a website similar to DigiKala at a very low price, but that is a mistake everybody makes. Repeating the experiences of others and hoping to reach the same results. However, you cannot achieve their results with the exact formulas they used.

Why do you think that is the case? Why can you not cross the path someone else did and reach the same destination they reached? It is because they crossed that path years ago, and everything has changed by now. You cannot copy their old ideas. Even they cannot succeed with their old formulas repeatedly.

If you take the same path others did, you will never achieve anything new. Your results might be similar to theirs at best. You do not need any guidelines and formulas to succeed in something. All you need to do is to pick a goal and start working on it. Your guidelines are unique to you and will be written as you move forward.

You might think that to find your true goals and unique journeys with this method, you will fail so many times that you would not have the energy to get back up again. That is correct. In this method, you will probably fail over and over again. But do not worry. You can extract energy from your failures as well!

In the next chapter, I will explain how failures can be energy-givers or even super-energisers.

Chapter Four: Success and Failure

Failure or success? That is not the question.

A trap named success

Failure is a blessing

The story of the great failure

Energy fluctuation or "The Summit Conquering" rule

How to overcome the energy-drainer known as success?

The magic power of failure

Failure at the deepest level of existence

Success or Failure? That is not the question!

When Shakespeare wrote, "To be or not to be, that is the question" in Hamlet, he could not have imagined that one day, his saying would go beyond the English language and get paraphrased in a book about energy. All of these strange turns of events are the works of the Energy Magician. He keeps pushing us to look at things from different perspectives.

Two soccer teams toss a coin to decide which team begins the match. As long as the coin is in the air, there is no way to predict which side it will land on: heads or tails?

When you start working on something, you have tossed a coin into the air. A coin with two sides: Success and Failure. What determines which side the coin lands on is your consistency.

When you start working on something, you cannot know where your hard work and preparations will lead you; all you know is that you want to voyage into the unknown. You want to succeed, so you tell yourself, "The road to success goes through failures." Your goal has been determined: "I will work hard to succeed in this new field."

What is your definition of success and failure? Is success a good happening, and failure a bad one? Can failure ever be a good thing? I believe that the Energy Magician can change old definitions and give new meanings to life.

The general definition of success is reaching the desired results after doing something.

You are sitting on a park bench in front of a pool and a fountain. Two people are running around the fountain. You look at their movements. They are very similar to each other; they are twins. The two brothers join you on the bench, tired and sweating. The first one says, "Did you see me break my yesterday's record and run three more rounds?"

The second brother smiles and says, "I finally managed to run 5 rounds like yesterday without losing my breath." The example of the twins proves that people can hope for different results from the same activities; it tells us that the concept of success is relative. What someone considers success can be a very ordinary achievement for somebody else. Therefore, we cannot say someone is successful, and someone else is not – we cannot compare people based on how successful they are. Again we can see that, "Success or failure, that is not the question!" There is no ultimate definition of success or failure – it is for the individuals to decide whether their results are successful or not.

If success is a relative concept that depends on individual expectations, what does failure mean?

Failure is generally defined as the opposite of success, not achieving the desired results after doing something.

Many factors can have a role in failures: childhood experiences, beliefs, currency fluctuations, economic depressions, losing funds, etc. What we want to consider here is the role of naysayers. These people do not believe in the Energy Magician, and all they can say, before even learning about the field, is 'No.' Another group of naysayers is made up of the mockers. If you share your dreams with the mockers, they activate the "mockery" energy-drainer and ridicule them. Naysayers hold the key to certain failures and constantly use their energy-drainers to take your energy away. They are always trying to stop you from starting something, and in case you do start, they underestimate you and tell you it is not possible all along the way. These people add to the hardships of the way; you must activate the seesaw of facing energy-drainers and get more determined every time they tell you something is not possible. Do not pay any attention to their negative words and take powerful steps to prove them wrong; that way, you can turn the naysayers into your energisers and prove to them that "Success or failure, that is not the question."

The Energy Magician can even turn failures into energy-givers.

Success books want to teach you how to always succeed and never fail. But how can somebody gain valuable experiences without failures and mistakes? Just as darkness gives meaning to light, failure gives meaning to success. Self-help books want to help you only succeed, but the Energy Magician book wants to show you how to turn failures into energy-givers. If you feel hopeless, shameful, and guilty after every failure, then you view failure as a bad thing and do not consider it a possible energy-giver.

The educational system teaches us that using the experiences of others, particularly successful people, can give us similar results and help us avoid failures, but real life says otherwise.

The experiences of others can inspire us to come up with new methods and see how internal energy guides others. However, if we try to copy the paths of others, the Energy Magician who loves creativity and challenge goes to sleep. Do not expect the Energy Magician to help you when you face unexpected obstacles in these situations; do you expect him to help you when you ignore him yourself? That is exactly when failure arrives. Copying the experiences of others cannot help you succeed. People do not have identical characteristics, circumstances, and timelines. Therefore, two people cannot get successful in the same way. There is no logical solution to rely on and follow. Find your own solutions through your internal energy.

Is life similar to how it used to be in the past? Can two people share identical conditions and time limits? Then how can their solutions be the same? Can two people even have identical perspectives, beliefs, and emotions? Then how are they supposed to share the same paths and solutions?

As you move toward your goals, the Energy Magician will prove to you that failure is not a sign of weakness.

Failure is not bad luck either; the Energy Magician can turn failure into a super-energiser.

If failure is an energy-giver, then, we have been fed the wrong definitions for years.

A trap named success

If your final goal is getting into college, what does the Energy Magician do after you achieve it? Do you congratulate yourself on getting into college and say I am done? Is such an achievement the end of your journey? If it is, then a simple success has swallowed all your energy.

Success can become an energy-drainer

Consider your achievements during your childhood and teenage days. Will you consider them success if you achieve them right now? Look at success during different time periods. Ten years ago, if my company had increased its sales 10 times over, I would have considered that a huge success. However, if that happens now, I will consider it a huge failure. What I consider to be desirable outcomes has changed, and I am aiming for grdrainer achievements today.

Humans lose their energy after achieving their goals. Great success can cause a false sense of confidence and pride, and that is a scary point on the road to success. Success convinces people to stay in their safety zone and do not risk what they have achieved. That is why people lose their energy after each success.

Many of us long for our successful days and wish we had managed to maintain our former states. Success has become our energy-drainer, and it is stopping us from moving forward and causing us to lose our current position, as well.

If you consider something as your ultimate goal, you will tell yourself, "I've reached my safety circle; why should I put myself at risk again?"

Achieving something is not the end of the journey.

Energetic people have a different definition of success. Instead of stopping after the first achievement, they take bigger risks and move toward bigger goals.

Failure is a blessing

You must have heard the saying, "Fear of the thing is worse than the thing itself." Fear of failure, as in fear of not achieving success as before, is an energy black hole and an illogical one, because everyone experiences failures many times. We should not think that high-energy people experience failure less than others or not at all; these people have just changed their outlook toward failure. Similarly, you can turn failure into an energy-giver with the help of the Energy Magician.

Failure means choosing a new path, not the end.

A failure is a natural event that gives us access to the deepest and most powerful type of internal energy.

Do not let failure take away your energy required to keep moving!

When you face an obstacle, you automatically get filled with more energy so that you can overcome it. As a natural obstacle against success, failure is a massive source of energy. After every failure, the Energy Magician gets more and more determined to use his powers; because he believes success to be overcoming obstacles.

Failing and getting back up provides you with enough power to take risks and start again, both of which are super-energisers. When someone fails, they learn to improve their opportunity-seeking abilities and increase their tolerance for problems. When you fail at something, it means you either have not discovered all your abilities or you are too influenced by damaging external agents. Failing can help you better understand the characteristics of what you are doing. Never consider your failures as endings. Failures are just new beginnings.

For many years, problems and pressures had been attacking me from all sides, and I was on the brink of bankruptcy. At that time, my partner had been arrested and locked up for financial reasons. I could not just sit around, wait for annihilation, and curse my bad luck. I had to do something. Something big. Despite all my problems, I was filled with energy and ready to face and overcome the obstacles. The interesting thing is that my energy levels at that time were so much higher than what I experienced after success. My energy levels had gotten high enough for me to overcome the giant ditches along the road. My Energy Magician kept reminding me that failure is just a new start, and the biggest achievements come from failures.

An ancient general was asked the secret to his conquests, and he answered, "A long time ago, I was severely defeated in a battle. I felt hopeless and shameful. I left my army and went to a secluded place to curse my fate and make a decision. I wanted to know if I should keep fighting or give up and go back to being a blacksmith in my hometown. At that moment, I saw an ant on the ground in front of me. It had picked a seed much heavier than itself and was taking it away. However, the seed was heavy and kept falling. Every time the seed would fall, the ant would pick it up again. It happened again and again until he managed to take it away. That ant taught me that I was mistaken to consider my first defeat shameful. So, I returned to my army to reorganise it, learn from my mistakes, recognise opportunities, and stand against problems. That is why I win every war now. I consider every defeat as the beginning of a great victory."

Failure is a unique experience as long as we learn from it and never repeat it.

The story of the great failure

If Japan had considered the nuclear bombing of Hiroshima and Nagasaki an irredeemable catastrophe, it would have never reached its current position. The nuclear bombing was a failure that Japan had to move on from, and it taught them to become so powerful that something like that would never happen again. The mentally and physically malformed children born after the bombing motivated the Japanese to make sure children never again experience disability due to events like war. Japan turned such a great catastrophe into an energy-giver, and through tireless efforts, became a centre of knowledge and industry.

Nearly thirteen years ago, two years after founding the company, we experienced a great and ruinous failure. Before long, we became bankrupt and owed a lot of money to banks, so much so that we could not even pay half of the debts if we sold all our belongings and assets. The worst part was that our debts grew larger by the day, and we could not even pay the interest on our bank loans anymore. Those were extremely hard days, and I remember every second of them as if it was just yesterday. I had to make life-changing decisions. Time used to fly by, and I could not waste a second of it. I had to do everything I could to change our circumstance for the better. I had to take risks and use their energy. I started my business using my savings and money borrowed from friends. To develop it further, I had my father's house as a security for the re-payment of the loans. My father had bought that house after a lifetime of hard work, and it was our family's only asset. The bank kept sending me warnings, and I had to find a solution and save my family's house. I did not want them to go homeless. During those hard days, I used to write down sentences that indicated my feelings on my phone. Those sentences are still very motivational and inspiring for me. I wrote one of them when trying to get my partner out of prison. I finally managed to arrange a meeting with one of the bank's board members. I sat in their office for over three hours just so I could speak with them for a few minutes. I wrote this sentence during those excruciating waiting hours: "I'm sitting in the office of Mr. … the head of the bank's board of directors. He had promised to not press charges and let my partner get out of jail but has changed his mind now. I am being destroyed. I have no idea what I'm supposed to do. May god help us."

Before going to sleep that same night, I wrote: "My partner is sleeping among thieves and murderers in prison right now, and I'm lying on this comfortable bed. I might be right there with him tomorrow night."

If our competitors and the marketplace found out about his arrest, we would have another catastrophe. Our company would lose all its credibility. I remember doing everything to prevent that. I took another risk and chose the last and only option. I borrowed a great amount of money to get him released from prison. That day I wrote: "My partner was released tonight, but it cost us another huge debt. May god save us."

You might be thinking that I should have just accepted defeat and stopped digging myself into a deeper hole. But no! I could not lose hope. I could not cause my family's ruin.

I once said something during an argument with a family member, something that nearly broke me. They told me, "Instead of trying to act like a grown-up, go do your job so you do not get arrested every other day and put the house at risk." I had no way out. I had no more moves to make. Nevertheless, I had to fix everything, no matter what it cost me. During that time, I was filled with so much power that I had trouble even recognising myself. I could not believe how I had managed to convince friends and acquaintances to trust me and lend me money. I spoke with so much determination and energy that my customers rarely turned me down. However, the results were still not enough. I worked late every night and woke up tired every morning after another night of nightmares. My entire body ached as if I had been performing heavy exercises. Some nights, I would fall asleep while working. I got arrested twice in my office due to bounced checks. Every day, I dreaded another bounced check and getting arrested again. What if they would not release me again? However, I stayed in the office for as long as

I could every day, trying to change things. On one of those days, I wrote:

"I will fight!

I will fight for my dad, who has gotten old from sadness. He has to see our success and feel at peace.

I will fight for my mother, who has worked for us all her life.

For my family's future

For my father's house

I will fight.

I will fight. Wait for me, happy days.

I will not fail."[3]

I would close my eyes and imagine a bright future for myself every night. Even though daydreaming was hard those days.

In my phone, I wrote: "The rays of hope appear in absolute darkness. Good days will come as long as you do not lose faith, keep patiently trying, and stay hopeful and smart." All of these problems at the same time can crush a 26-year-old person. I went to bed and woke up every day feeling like I was being

---

[3] These are the exact words I wrote down. It still surprises me that I wrote such things.

chased by a wolf. Troubles kept following me, and my only thought was fighting this "great failure". I call it my great failure because so many problems at once are too much for a 26-year-old. But despite all of that, I never gave up. I did not want to lose. I could not imagine giving up for even a second. It was not just about me and my fate; my family's future was at risk. I kept asking myself, "What would happen to them if I failed?" My failure and my love for my family became two super-energisers, filling me with energy and determination.

If I had to find one reason for my success at such a young age, I would choose my great failure.

Discover failure's energizing secret.

Consider the hardest moments of your life, the ones you considered to be the end, the ones with no solution and no way out. Didn't you have a ray of hope deep in your heart during those moments? Didn't the light of hope fill your entire being? Didn't it tell you, "You still have a chance; you can do this?" I am sure you wanted to believe those hopeful messages, and you were suddenly filled with energy and took an oath that you would win. You swore that you were on a new day, and you would find a solution to overcome all your troubles. Things could have been harder.

Your secret powers do not show themselves during normal and comfortable conditions.

You can only recognise your true self when your internal energy is released. Nothing can stop your growth, then. You are a ship that is moving across life's unpredictable ocean. You might face storms and unwanted situations any day. Storms that can cause you great failures. These storms are telling you to constantly build and rebuild yourself and increase your energy through your troubles. After overcoming your problems, you will be surprised by how much you have changed. You will wonder, "Am I really this new and powerful person?"

If you study the lives of energetic historical figures, you will see that they faced dark days, unsolvable problems, and successive failures, as well. However, they faced them with a different mind-set.

After discovering that the earth is not the centre of the world but a planet orbiting a star, Galileo was called a pagan and threatened with a death sentence. After he was forced to recant his claims in a court, Galileo said, "Eppur si muove," which was the Italian for "And yet it moves". What he had meant was, "even though I recanted my claims, the earth still moves around the sun."

Do you think Galileo succeeded or failed? In reality, every event is just some energy. The nature of the energy does not get affected by any labels we might put on it. We interpret and label events based on our perspectives. If results match our expectations, we call them successes. If they do not, we call them failures. However, these names are insignificant compared to the energy of the events.

Forbes magazine claims that 70 percent of American billionaires have experienced at least three big bankruptcies.

Failures are energy sources that can be used if people take risks after they fail. Taking risks after failures means facing your failure and attempting to use it as a launching pad toward success. The more risk-tolerant people are after failures, the more chances of success they have.

Success can never provide you with as much energy as failure does.

Energy fluctuation or "The Summit Conquering" rule

If you discover the hidden energy of failures, they will uncover your path toward success. After succeeding, energy levels fluctuate and decrease, but according to the law of energy balance, that energy is not gone; it has just been transformed.

Imagine that you have decided to conquer the summit of a mountain. You climb steep and dangerous paths. Steep angles make you nervous; what if you fall?! You climb the mountain despite all the hardships and reach the summit. As you proudly look down at the earth from the summit, you enter a new energy cycle, because it is time for you to climb down to the ground. This time, the journey is easier. Since you have achieved your goal and conquered the summit, you face a decrease in energy and motivation. You need a small amount of energy to climb down, and as you get closer to the ground and your safety zone, your energy levels keep decreasing further. When you reach the base of the mountain, there is no sign of all the energy you used to have.

What we have discussed so far have all been new perspectives toward success and failure. Now, I have a simple task for you: review your past failures and successes and your reactions, thoughts, and feelings about them. Now, look at them from your new perspective.

How to overcome the energy drainer known as success?

To maintain your energy levels after succeeding, paying attention to the following rules is necessary:

1. Small successes and failures are meaningless in creating a better and happier life. Each success must be considered a stepping stone toward a bigger success, like the links in a chain.

   You might be wondering, "If somebody achieved their biggest goal and did not have any bigger ones, what happens to their internal energy? Can they save themselves from life's stormy ocean?"

   Firstly, people can only have the energy and determination to fight obstacles when they are constantly setting goals for themselves. Secondly, no goal can ever be someone's final goal. According to the conquering summit rule, you must always set a bigger goal for yourself, or you will lose your energy and move backward.

2. Never magnify a success. Always remember that you are much more important than your achievements. Do not let an achievement make you so joyful and ecstatic that you forget about your other goals.

3. Understand the role of chance and people in your achievements. If you achieve something as a team, give credit to your teammates. Most people give all the credit for achievement to themselves and completely ignore everyone and everything else. On the other hand, whenever they fail, all the blame goes to bad luck and other people.

4. Always remember that growth is more important than success. Thus, plan for personal growth just like you plan for success. This is because if your achievement is bigger than your personality, you will lose it.

The closest word to what I consider to be "Growth" is "Energy". Instead of focusing on your results, focus on your growth.

5. Think about how much of your achievements you owe to God's grace and blessing. How effective do you consider God's will in your successes? If you believe that you would have never achieved anything if God had not been kind to you, you would never get arrogant. You will always be selfless and thankful. Maybe the conditions you experience are divine tests. Their purpose might be to test you when you are at your peak.

6. Do not think you will be free and comfortable after you have achieved your goals. After achieving them, you must keep them by moving forward to new goals.

The Magic Power of Failure

The amount of energy you can get from failures is directly related to how hard the situation is and how deteriorated you are to keep moving. All boxers endure heavy blows during matches. They get back up over and over again and keep fighting.

If you asked professional boxers what helped them win their toughest opponent, they would talk about the single heaviest and most painful blow they had received. Failures are the punches life throws at us; they turn us into champions.

If you want to turn your failures into super-energisers that move you on the path toward growth, do not exaggerate them. Some people try to earn themselves some sympathy by exaggerating their problems. They even sympathise with themselves. What they do not understand is that their actions are activating a massive and undefeatable black hole. Exaggerating failures and receiving sympathy takes their energy away and makes sure they do not continue with their journey. Then, they will truly become failures.

For example, we all know people who exaggerate their failures in romantic relationships and consider themselves to be the victims. They enjoy being sympathised with and do not try to improve or keep walking down the same paths. If you want to grow in all aspects of life, refrain from exaggerating your problems. That is the only way to enter the Improvement Cycle.

The improvement cycle means starting, failing, accepting the failure, analysing it and learning from it, and taking risks again. The base of this cycle is accepting failures. We had always been told success is an energy-giver, and failure is an energy-drainer. We did not know how much energy failure has to offer. However, the Energy Magician uses failures to release your internal energy as long as you get back up and take risks again after every failure.

Never underestimate the power of failure in releasing your energy.

Failure at the deepest level of existence

As you know, atoms are the smallest particles of elements. Each atom has a nucleus, filled with neutrons and protons surrounded by electrons. Many forces exist between the particles of an atom, and the nucleus is so dense with energy that all the heavy particles inside it remain together. When the nucleus splits into two or more nuclei, all that energy is released. In nuclear physics, that process is called nuclear fission. According to Einstein's law, when a nucleus with a big atomic number splits, some of its mass turns into energy. One nuclear fission experiment can produce as much energy as 200 million electronvolts. On the other hand, burning a piece of coal produces only a few electronvolts of energy. That is why this technology is used to create electricity in nuclear implants or cause destruction with weapons.

Thus, failure in the deepest level of existence can produce such a massive amount of energy. That energy would have remained inaccessible if the nucleus had not been split.

We have told you that failures can release a lot of energy in people, as well. They can use that energy to get back up, take risks, and move forward. The bigger and deeper the failure, the more internal energy and potential it releases inside you. When a failure runs deep into your heart and mind and happens in your "nucleus", the released internal energy can help you take the biggest steps of your life and achieve your biggest goals. If you get back up after such a failure, your growth and success are guaranteed.

Chapter Five: Ownership and Energy Levels

Energy and the level of life

What you have and have not

The sense of ownership and its impacts on energy levels

Please do not be a bittern

How does the energy of extra belongings get freed?

Variations in energy levels

The relationship between the level of life and energy levels

Energy and the level of life

In this chapter, the impacts of the level of our lives on our energy levels will be investigated. Before anything, we should refer to the experience of the COVID-19 pandemic. When the disease got spread, the fear of the ominous virus and the calamities that people and their loved ones could face suddenly diminished the energy levels of everybody around the world. This, in turn, reduced the level of life. Even the global economy faced unimaginable crises. Fundamental changes occurred in working and moneymaking, and many people changed how they lived. Many people blamed the hard times they experienced as the reason for their misfortune, and they felt their energy levels constantly decreased without considering whether they adapted to the changes in conditions or not. Moreover, they could not perceive the level of their internal energy when their level of life got reduced: whether they remained depressed and dejected and waited for the situation to change. The difficult and strange circumstances in the COVID-19 era reduced energy levels, and this loss of energy influenced everyone's life. With this introduction, we define the level of life as the quality of life that is determined by factors like the rate of monthly income, the level of one's occupation and satisfaction with it, everyday expenditures, the quality of instruments one uses, and, particularly, our luxurious attitudes. In any difficult situation, we can overcome any crisis, threat, and disorder if our energy levels are high. Thus, the positive effects of that can be observed in the level of one's life. No doubt, energy levels influence people's levels of life, but the relationship is not necessarily a two-way one, and each individual might respond in a different way.

No matter who you are, how smart and hard-working you are, what is your academic degree, or how many specialised courses and training programs you have passed, your energy levels influence them all. It is at this point that the issue of energy levels and their relationship with the level of life comes under the spotlight. Some people take the bus to commute every day, while others feel energy losses until they buy the most luxurious model of the car they like. Sometimes, not having something and concentrating on the lack of it reduces one's energy levels considerably, and the loss exceeds the energy required to achieve the same thing.

A farmer looks at his neighbour's farm from dusk to dawn instead of working on his own farm and experiences undesirable feelings by observing the neighbour's endeavours, the constant growth of the crops, and his efforts to constantly improve the products. He yearns for whatever other people have without considering the circumstances in which he lives. It is natural such yearning takes a lot of energy from him. He wastes his time during the cultivation months and regrets it when he looks at his negligible harvest. An interesting point is that he knows he has spent less energy (or no energy) on his work compared to his neighbour. Perhaps you criticise the farmer and blame him for his inability to harvest suitably. Nevertheless, many of us may have performed the same behaviour during a period of our lives. Perhaps we have not acknowledged the value of our belongings and looked at what others have by thinking that "the grass is always greener on the other side of the fence," and this has depleted our energy completely. If you turn what you do not have into what you desire to have, you will stop losing your energy. Never let the feeling of regret about anything you do not have diminish the energy required to continue your endeavours. Take a look at the experience of people who failed several times in their lives. They lost everything, and even their former status got shaken. However, they maintained the level of their energy and exploited failure as an energising factor. They stood up once again and started afresh. Thus, they reached even better positions as they did not let their level of life determine their energy levels in any circumstances.

Right now, make a list of what you do not have and start endeavouring to achieve them if they are really important and necessary to you. In this way, you can destroy the black hole of energy.

What you have and have not

What is the most significant property that you own? Suppose that one day you are informed that you can travel to another space, but you are allowed to just take the most significant property that you have. In such a situation, what will you take? Perhaps you will be forced to abandon many things so that you can take the one and only thing you desire most. Your most remarkable belonging is your energy. You can achieve whatever you desire when you are full of energy. Now, focus on your life and past: how do you look at what you have and do not have? Does concertation on what you do not have increase or decrease your energy? Imagine that the cell phone of a woman who is madly in love with photography is damaged, and its photos are not as good as before. On the other hand, she does not have enough money to buy a new phone or make hers fixed. The natural and unavoidable reaction is that she gradually loses a lot of energy because of the absence of a professional cell phone. On the other hand, the energy required to buy a new phone is much less than that.

The energy that is lost when dealing with routine issues is much higher than the energy required to achieve great results and goals; for instance, the energy lost because of a damaged mobile phone or not having the latest model of that is very much higher than whatever is necessary to be spent on buying a phone. In addition, the energy that we lose when we cannot buy something due to increased prices is much higher than the energy we need to purchase that commodity. Examples such as this are plentiful. The everyday issues of life our dissatisfaction with the neighbourhood where we live, concerns about renewing our house rent contracts, unending disagreement with our parents, and our inability to study in what we desire – to name but a few – deplete your energy in a way that you do not have anything to spare in the way to achieve your goals.

To hold your energy at high levels, you only need to maintain it and utilise it in the appropriate paths.

When I was a university student, I did not have a car and used public transportation. To be honest, I never thought that if I had taken a taxi instead of buses, I could have travelled much more comfortably. Moreover, I did not think about whether I could pay for the taxis or purchase a car. Now that I look back at the period, I notice that I never thought about what "I did not have," and this did not take any energy from me.

Bill Gates is one of the most energetic people in the world. In his interviews, he repeatedly emphasised the fact that he never bought a new car and was used to second-hand ones. Bill Gates is not a miser. Indeed, he did not care about the model of the care he drove. What is interesting is that ordinary people act exactly the opposite - i.e., they spend a huge amount of their energy on their everyday life and the improvement of the quality of their life. Take a look at the lives of energetic people who live around you, and you will notice that they do not think about what they lack. It is not that they assign no importance to driving the latest model of their favourite car. Rather, it is very important for them, but this is not their priority. Their minds are occupied by much more important matters, and they spend their energy to achieve them. What would you choose to wear in front of a reporters' camera if you were Mark Zuckerberg? In response to questions like, "Don't you have another T-shirt?" or "Why do you wear a plain T-shirt for most ceremonies," Zuckerberg said, "Such work is time-consuming and takes a lot of energy. I really don't have extra time to think about what I should wear!"

In your opinion, what prompts us to call a level of life luxurious, average, or low? You can find hundreds of pages offering information about luxurious cars, houses, etc., with just a simple search on social media. You experience feelings of dissatisfaction, disappointment, and regret about what others have by comparing the level of your life with such instances. Consequently, you lose your energy. Major international corporations provide us with wrong definitions of the level of life and its relationship with our internal energy through global advertising and the promotion of consumerism. They want us to believe that having more properties and owning the most expensive things increases our energy levels and even satisfaction and happiness. Moreover, they want to induce the thought that "you can attain the position of the perfect human by owning more things." The culture of consumerism has prompted many people to spend their energy on their own things from dusk to dawn during their whole lives, and this has trapped societies in the cycle of "wasting energy to own more, more, and even more." In such cultures, something that a person has at the present moment is not valuable, and their levels of life are not considered desirable. Thus, humans are turned into a printing press that creates title deeds. In this way, they are devoured by a monster called the energy black hole, forget about living, and never take their time to enjoy what they have collected.

Do you want to improve the quality of your life? First, you need to accept that in most cases, "earning more" cannot increase the level of your energy, and "losing" does not lead to any energy loss. It should not sound surprising that the very losses can sometimes increase your energy levels. Instead of concentrating on what you do not have, think about your present level of energy. Do you have enough energy to move toward the achievement of your goals? Have you recognised energy-drainers? Do you know what you should do to regain your energy whenever you experience energy loss? If you consider such matters, you will certainly stay on your path, and you will achieve your great goals full of energy and strength in no time at all.

The sense of ownership and its impact on energy levels

In your opinion, what are the most important things a person should have? A very spacious house or the neighbourhood in which you live? Do you assign significant value to the price and model of the car you drive?

Nowadays, we seek to own the "most expensive" things more than ever in history. The culture tells us, "I can appear worthier by owning the most expensive ones!" The Best, the Most Expensive, and the Most Luxurious are relative adjectives, and there is always something that is better, more expensive, and more luxurious than the previous ones. Human beings become greedier when they own more things. In other words, the well of greed can never be filled up. When the monster of greed wakes up, it cannot be surpassed forever. In Persian mythology, the monster of greed has been introduced as one of the allies of Ahriman. Thus, the monster devours all creatures, even its commander – Ahriman – in the apocalypse. When there is nothing more, it devours itself!

The majority of the youth in our society believe that people with more property are more successful. In addition, they assume that they should be equipped with many things from the beginning to achieve great advances. However, they do not know that such attitudes deprive them of the opportunities and experiences of making a start, risking, and benefitting from the joys of life. Thus, growth in any field is not determined by luxurious ownership, but by your energy levels. Two remarkable reasons that waste your energy are the feeling of ownership over something that belongs to you and your endeavours to protect and maintain it. These two characteristics consume a significant portion of your energy so that you may not exploit your life. People with the above characteristics always live with the fear of losing their belongings.

Ownership is an energy-drainer if it is not understood properly.

Life incidents are unpredictable. We do not know when we will achieve or lose something. Can we guarantee that we will own something on this planet a second later? In a very old story, I read that a very influential and wealthy man did his best to seize a piece of land owned by a poor man and finally achieved his goal. He built a spacious and magnificent palace on that land and invited a lot of guests to visit the place. The guests arrived and waited for their honourable host to welcome them. However, the man did not appear! The governor was one of the guests. Everybody expected their host to come forward and pay due respect to the governor, but there was no sign of the man. The governor went to the rich man's room and ordered some people to open the door. As soon as the door was open, the governor and the people around him saw that the host was dead on his chair! By considering the strange developments of life, is it not better to modify the concept of ownership and say that you own what you use and get energy from its presence? In other words, the only things that belong to you are the ones you use, the very things God Almighty has given to you as your "daily share." Anything that is saved and not used is an energy-drainer. If you want to stop losing your energy, you need to transform your sense of owning things into using them. This can increase your energy unbelievably. Extra apartments are left empty, money is deposited somewhere and is not spent, and hundreds of similar cases do not belong to you and are inherited by others when you die. Merely owning things turns you into the guardian of your properties. The extreme sense of ownership and attachment turn you into something that is owned by your properties; in other words, such properties become your owners. Nevertheless, the sense of ownership is not limited to materials – this sense is too energy-consuming in an emotional relationship. A mother who feels ownership toward her children is always worried about losing them. Couples who feel a sense of ownership toward one another consume all their energy because of their fears of losing one another and controlling the other party. However, when an emotional relationship is not based on a sense of ownership, every moment of it can be full of joy. In this way, the same amount of energy that is consumed on controlling the other party and the fear of losing them can be used to construct a lasting, intimate, and convenient relationship.

Profound attachment and dependence prompt you to stick to your properties and consume all your energy on extending, protecting, and maintaining them.

Please do not be a bittern

Bitterns are birds that live by the sea but do not drink even a single drop of the water as they fear the water will be depleted. The life of a bittern reflects the story of people who store all their properties, do not use them, and do not let others get benefit from them. Bitterns never make use of the joys of their lives. The sense of ownership is a mental trap that consumes your energy, attracts you, and makes you addicted. You should not forget that a single breath can put an end to all attachments and dependencies. If you have a villa that you do not use, you are not its actual owner. You are just a guardian who consumes energy protecting the property. All surplus properties, from clothes to the most expensive things you can imagine are burdens on your shoulders. In storerooms of some houses, extra commodities that can supply a whole new house are kept. They are stores so that one day, they may become useful, though such days never come. As a personal experience, when I changed the decoration of the house and changed the furniture, I put an ad online on second-hand stores to sell the old furniture – that was because I believed I had to get myself relived from something I did not need so that I may not waste my energy on it.

Rich people are not the only ones who become attached to materials and their properties. I have witnessed this energy-drainer in many people with little wealth. I know a person who is average in terms of his socioeconomic condition, but he has had a strong sense of ownership over his negligible properties since the days of his youth. Many years ago, he started a severe dispute with a friend on a piece of land until he started to suffer from Alzheimer's disease. Then, though he could not remember even his family members, he still talked about the dispute and suffered from it! That was because the energy-eating sense of ownership had penetrated the innermost layers of his unconscious mind.

The sense of ownership slows down humans on their way toward success and acts like weights attached to their feet. When you attain something for which you feel a sense of ownership, the number of weights increases. You buy apartments in several locations in your city, though you do not use any of them or do not offer them for rent. Even if you may not visit them once a month, this type of ownership is something that wastes a lot of your energy.

The sense of ownership becomes damaging when you become attached to something beyond your need.

If you have properties that have made you into unpaid guardians, you need to quickly identify the energy-eating sense of ownership and take steps to release the energy trapped within such properties.

How can the energy trapped by surplus properties be released?

a. Donation is one of the ways to release the burden of the surplus properties that turn you into their guardians. Donate one-fifth of your properties. If you can do this, energies can no longer devour you. The energy provided by donation counteracts the one subtracted by the sense of ownership. Donation means giving something that you love most. If it is hard to donate valuable things, try to start with smaller ones. Donate your favourite T-shirt to someone. Give your perfume to your sister. Using such simple practices, giving up the most valuable things becomes easier.

Donation requires courage.

b. Taking risks is another way to release the energy of surplus properties. Such properties act as the pyramid of success to you. Risk half your properties – i.e., use them to start something that you always feared to begin. When I was a small child (around 9 or 11), I always told my father to sell our spacious three-story house and use the money to start a business so we could move to a smaller house. Though my father did not take the risk, I did it when I was twenty-three. Then, I deposited the money in a bank a started a business that witnessed lots of failures and risks and helped me move toward growth and advancement.

Face your fears headlong so that the very act can give you energy. What awaits you if you do that? Will you fail? Well, what is wrong with failing?

What will you lose? In the previous chapters, it was argued that failure can be invigorating.

A while ago, one of my friends visited me to get counsel and told me he could not choose one of the following two options on how to use his surplus money: whether to sell his only car and start a business with the collected money or use the surplus money to buy a better car and enjoy it. He feared that if he started a business with surplus money, he would fail and lose all his savings. My response was that anyone who takes a risk to start a new business or develop an existing one receives more energy than someone who only thinks about hoarding more money.

When you take risks, you do your best to succeed, and the very thing increases your energy. However, when you do not take risks and try to collect more properties, you are always fearful of losing whatever you have. Such worries and fears take a lot of your energy, and these can become obstacles against more significant leaps in the future. In this way, you become conservative persons who cannot introduce transformations into your lives.

During the time I experienced a significant failure, I sold my car to pay my employees' wages. It felt very painful at first, since I had become accustomed to having a personal car. However, I sold it with no regret. I had to give it up as a sacrifice to achieve my goals. I had nothing to lose, and this made me work harder. Perhaps selling my car was a turning point that paved my way from the hardest days toward success and higher positions. I clearly remember that something inside me whispered, "now that you have risked everything you have, you need to fight with all your power and achieve success."

Perhaps you have to reduce the quality of your life so that you can achieve more success in your business and goals. If you do that, you have won greatly.

c. Invest in yourself

A very attractive activity is to spend your surplus capital on yourself. Participating in various courses like specialised occupational programs, artistic endeavours like music or painting, travel, and exercise are an investment that you make in yourself. When you learn and experience something new, you spend your surplus capital, and at the same time, transform the energy hidden in the spent capital into your internal energy.

As humans become more interested in hoarding materials, they are more likely to be damaged by that as they take fewer risks in their lives and lose the power to donate. My suggestion is that you should keep off hoarding surplus materials as much as possible, since dependence on them wastes your energy. However, this does not mean that you should not try harder to make more money or that you should be content with the minimum level. I mean, you should be aware that the negative addiction to "hoarding" does not prevent you from living; to put it in better terms, you should endeavour to receive positive energies from your properties.

Perhaps you assume that "saving" is the same as hoarding without using it, as the two terms are considered equal in popular culture. The answer is that saving is rooted in fear: the fear of losing, poverty, and plight. Such fears strengthen the sense of ownership by saving, and the saved materials become factors that consume your energy. If I need to choose between being a fearful, wealthy man, and a courageous, risk-taking person who is average in terms of his economic condition, I choose the latter, as courage is an energy-giver. Whatever you use turns into energy, and whatever you save for an unspecified date turns into a burden that slows down and hinders your movement. Owning real estates is not considered an important asset in modern businesses; rather, intellectual properties and specialties are more valuable and are considered the most significant assets of business enterprises. Banks in the developed world do not guarantee their loads by requiring properties. The very fact proves that you do not need to have surplus properties at all.

At the moment, we do not have surplus properties in our company. My friends often advise me to invest in real estate using the surplus revenues of the company, but I do not own any properties other than the company site. Indeed, I live in a rented house. Banks no longer require title deeds to give loans to us and trust our remarkable performance. Thus, I risk whatever I earn and find new challenges for the company and myself.

I develop the company in this manner as I do not fear any failure and losing my capital.

Variations in energy levels

People are divided into three levels in terms of their energy levels:

The first class includes people who view failures and losses as energising factors. Whenever they lose something, not only do they not fall back and become disappointed, but they become invigorated, retain their power, and move forward, stronger than before. Their past experiences have taught them how to become energised by whatever they lack, and even their lower levels of life.

The energy levels of such people are usually high because they seek to gain energy from whatever they get their hands on. Good and bad events are meaningless in their minds; any event has an energising message that has to be seen as an opportunity. In this way, they are not threatened by any energy-eating happening. Their focus is not on what they lack but on how to utilise whatever they have. Thus, they have transformed whatever they lack from "regrets" into "goals." They analyse what they lack according to their actual needs, target their essential and most remarkable needs, and eliminate anything that is surplus to their needs. Then, they move toward their goals with enough energy. They have learned how to focus their energy on starting and taking risks, and it is no surprise if they attain what they desire with the minimum loss of energy.

The second class includes people who are used to regard whatever they have as small and insufficient. They do not get much energy from what they have as they typically concentrate on others' properties. They envy other people's properties and spend their energy on achieving similar things. However, when they attain them, they cannot get enough energy from them. Their behaviour becomes stranger when they choose a new goal to pursue. They do not fight for their actual needs and desires. When we look at them from a distance, they look rather successful. They have everything and are hard-working, though they lack any signs of satisfaction, happiness, and joy. They have become machines that can just hoard money, wealth, and properties. When they lose something or fail, they immediately feel energy loss and unhappiness. The life of such people is constant competition with no winner. In this way, they become animals whose only goal is to collect more wealth. They gain the energy and motivation to win from their feelings of regret, envy, and pity about whatever others have. Unfortunately, the majority of people around the world who have little achievements belong to this group.

The third class includes people who are exactly the opposite of the first class. Such people do not get any energy from their belongings. They cannot see them, and consequently, never experience the joy of possessing something. Moreover, they act strangely toward whatever they do not have as they focus on things that they do not have and turn their minds into perpetual energy-eating machines. They unconsciously waste a significant portion of their energy every day. Thus, no matter how much energy they receive, their waste it and always energy shortage. Their energies get depleted during failures or losses as they consider obstacles as failures or destruction. As they always look at what they do not have, they never live in the moment.

Such stress and worries waste a lot of their energy, and this energy reduction brings about a series of issues for them. Various events can be energising or enervating. In other words, the manner of viewing challenges, events, and even life routines results in energy variations. You should not believe that you are born with bad luck. You just need to change your attitude so that stones can be transformed from obstacles into beautiful pavement and make your passage more pleasant.

Do you want to become a member of the first class? Then you need to stop looking at whatever other people have and acknowledge the value of your own belongings. Turn whatever you lack into goals; this will reduce the energy you need to move on and start afresh. Assume that each loss and failure is a necessary step to earn more in the near future. Do not let your energy levels go down.

The relationship between the level of life and energy levels

So far, we have talked about the level of life relative to energy levels; now, do you think the two are directly related to each other? Is it the case that when you enhance your level of life, your energy levels get increased? Do you think a person who is entangled in poverty consumes less energy than Bill Gates? Do not laugh at my question! I was completely serious. You should not be surprised that people suffering from poverty and similar problems in their lives spend a lot of energy on their regrets and other problems of their lives, and this wasted energy is not at all smaller than what Bill Gates spent on developing Microsoft! While the former has lost a significant portion of energy to energy-eating factors, the latter has spent his energy on the path of growth and advancement. Sometimes, directing the magical energy toward a convenient and energising path just depends on changing one's perspective toward issues and events and paying more attention to one's energy. Be sure that poverty and plight consume as much energy as whatever is required for growth and excellence. Poverty is an energy black hole. There are many rich people with low energy levels. They live in luxurious and magnificent houses, but they have cold and soulless families. Children play with their phones, the mother watches TV, and the father is barely at home! No matter how high the energy level is in such a house, it lacks any energy currents. The opposite can be true, as well: in a university dorm, several students are highly energetic, despite the multitude of limitations that kind of life exerts on them. As a result, ideas like the creation of "Google" or "Facebook" are introduced there. In most cases, there is a direct and significant relationship between the two parameters – i.e., the level of life and energy levels. In other words, we should not expect that an increase in the level of life will lead to a proportionate increase in energy levels. Indeed, we should not conclude that gaining more wealth is synonymous with an increase in our energy levels. Sometimes, people with lower levels of life enjoy a high level of energy. You have certainly experienced that when you buy a more spacious house or a better car, the change introduces more motivation and energy into your life in the short run. Nevertheless, everything becomes ordinary after a while, and buying an even bigger house may not produce the same enthusiasm. The reason is clear: the only thing that is directly related to our energy levels is how we look at life; in other words, you can only increase your energy levels when you change your attitudes and deal with what you have and lack and your sufferings by taking a new perspective.

The level of life is not worth so much as to become an energy-eating factor, and you just need to watch your energy levels. Do not imagine that your energy levels will be enhanced when you resolve your economic issues. Never let routine problems consume your energy and take you away from your paths. Do not forget that changing the level of life takes a lot of time, but changes in energy levels can be maintained more rapidly by changing your attitudes. The only thing that can save a difficult life is being equipped with high energy levels.

If you manage to make positive changes in your energy levels, you will be able to change the level of your life in the way you desire. Moreover, you may even attain such energy levels in the level of your life becomes an insignificant matter.

Chapter Six: The Energy

Energy exchange

The secret to the energy equation

The sensors of the energy

energy needs to be managed

Reinforcement the group energy

The golden rule

Power Castle energy

Energy exchange

Social existence is one of the main characteristics of human beings, and living in the quarantine during the pandemic showed how they suffered passivity without social relationships. On this basis, energy is defined in terms of individual and group states, and the two states can influence one another. We talked about people's internal energies in the previous chapter, and now we are going to discuss the group energy of a sports team, a musical band, a theatrical group, a production or advertising team, or a company doing imports and exports. Social life is accompanied by the perpetual exchange of energy. As the harmony between the members of a group helps them to achieve their goals, the energy of individual people can be accumulated to produce a group form of energy. Group energy determines the overall outcome of a group or team. The exchange of individual and group energies is always active, and the two are fed by one another. In this way, each individual's energy influences the energy of their society, and the energy of society is a combination of the energy of all people who are involved in constant energy exchange.

A friend was telling me that he had entered a new workplace. Every morning when he arrived, he saw that every place was shining, and a beam of energy and motivation to spend a good working day surged the hall and every room. All of this arose due to the manager's behaviour. The manager was full of energy, transferred motivation and satisfaction wherever she stepped in. Her behaviours, orders, and plans would turn the workplace into a dynamic and invigorating atmosphere. However, barely an hour later, the situation completely changed! I did not have the spirit to work there anymore. Then, I just waited for the hour to end my work, or I hoped the manager would send me to do some business outside that place. The change would take place as soon as a colleague entered the room and started to complain about heavy traffic, red lights, last night's rainfall, low salary, and his headache the night before! He complained about nearly anything that could be imagined. As soon as he came, all of the energy of the morning disappeared, and we had a boring and depressing workplace until the end of that working day. On the other hand, we became filled with joy whenever he took a day off. This very clear story shows how the energy levels of the personnel working in a workplace depend on one another, and the arrival of a powerful energy-drainer can easily change the direction of each person's (and later, the whole group's) energy. In this way, if an energiser enters a group, the person is absorbed in the cycle of the group energy of the environment and enhances the energy level of the group because people are placed in the cycle of the group energy of their environments.

The FIFA World Cup Qualifiers are being held, and if your national team is placed at the top of its group, it will be qualified for the games. You have focused completely on the match and angrily shout at the players whenever they make a mistake or lose the ball. Assume that your brother or sister says, "Why are you so excited? It will either will or lose! Is the difference between them so significant?"

Without taking your eyes off the screen, you say, "You are too stupid to understand the situation!" Your sibling leaves the room indifferently and does not come back until you shout, "Hooray, we are in the World Cup now!" You get dressed to go and join the people on the streets who are shouting and dancing happily. You ask your sibling to accompany you. Before long, you see your sibling has absorbed the enthusiasm of the people.

In your opinion, what has happened to the person's sibling? Yes, he/she has been influenced by group energy. He/she has not been able to resist the exchange of energy and has absorbed the enthusiasm of other people. The very group energy is the most significant factor in actualising many social-historical movements in various eras. An individual's energy is connected with the energy of other individuals and the whole society. When smaller communities are connected with larger ones, a "global energy network" is constructed, and we join the network by getting connected to one another.

The secret to the energy equation

Our energy is always influenced by the energy of the team and group members and the inhabitants of cities, countries, and even all the people around the world. Various family, occupational, and cultural – name but a few – constant communications determine our energy levels. If you review the fluctuation of your energy during various hours before and after each interaction or presence in a group, you will notice that interacting with others is an exchange to maintain equilibrium between internal and external energies and reveals the secret to the energy equation. An individual's internal energy is not separate from the environment and others, and such energies always influence the energy of an individual. Variations in the level of group energy change an individual's energy levels.

Recall a day when you were in great trouble. Review the circumstances. Tour friend was with you during the whole period you were dealing with the problem. Your energy at the time was remarkably influenced by your friend's energy. Recall your family atmosphere. Investigate the effect of variations in your energy levels on them. No doubt, your family members had certain reactions influenced by your energy levels. Energised people are typically more attractive to other people because energy is highly attractive. As an example, we miss such people more readily than others. It is as if they supply our internal food. In this way, the intensity and quality of your energy influence groups larger than the family.

The sensors of understanding the group energy

If we always want to maintain a high level of energy, we should strengthen the energy sensor and achieve an accurate understanding of the quality and quantity of energy at any moment. Energy sensors help us to understand our energy levels and regulate their relationship with the group energy of the environment where we live. Perhaps you assume that the perceptions made by our senses are instruments for perceiving and assessing energy levels, but perceiving the energy that exists in the environment and individuals is not necessarily conducted using our senses. That is because you may perceive a person's energy of happiness or excitement without observing smiles on their faces. In talking about perceiving internal energies, the responsibility is carried out by the activation of the internal sensors of energy perception. The sensors are something like insight, intuition, or the third eye.

It is a common experience that when we enter some place, we perceive the quality of its energy; for instance, we have noticed a heavy environment without knowing what happened before our arrival or being informed by others. Later, we are informed about an unhappy occurrence like a dispute or the arrival of bad news, and this confirms our sensory perceptions of the group energy of the environment. The opposite also holds true. In other words, you arrive at some place and feel something pleasant and enter a harmonious relationship with others present in the environment. We experience such perceptions repeatedly in various situations. In the book "Rescuing Dad" by Pete Johnson, the protagonist's parents go into the kitchen to talk after a lengthy dispute. A few minutes later, the girl looked at her brother and said, "It is as if the smell of their reconciliation has filled the air, hasn't it?" The boy agreed and said that it was strange because he sensed the same smell in the air, as well. No doubt, reconciliation has no real smell to be detected by smell. Rather, the above discussion refers to a current of energy that flows around and changes the surrounding environment. It was because of the same sense that the children in the above story perceived the sensory results of the conversation between their parents. In other words, the children's energy sensors had perceived changes in the type of energy that flowed in the environment.

Does the environment take on the group energy, or are the messages perceived based on people's moods? What happens around you to activate energy sensors? Perhaps the manner of perceiving the energy that flows in the environments cannot be explained, but perceiving the energy level of a group or an individual is a daily experience - like eating – that is repeated constantly. Imagine you are sitting in a room with some of your colleagues and are busy doing some work. Like any other day, you begin your work by greeting your colleagues, starting your computer up, and reviewing anything that should be performed and followed up. Suddenly, you raise your head and say to your colleague, "You are not in the mood today!"

He smiles and responds, "Why are you asking? I'm fine." You cannot explain how you experienced that feeling. Moreover, his behaviour has not reflected any signs of unhappiness. Then, how have you noticed his low spirit? Actually, your energy sensors enabled you to attain an updated understanding of your colleague's internal energy. Moreover, energy sensors specify the dominant energy of a group.

The magic of group energy

If the members of a successful team are asked, "What was the reason for their success," they respond, "We just stayed together and performed the decisions we had made." When the members of a group come together to carry out a joint task, the magical energy of each person becomes connected with that of others. Then, a team of energy magicians is formed; in other words, several energy sources come together to form a new source. The energy that is released from this source far exceeds the sum of the members' energy. The association of energy magicians utilises each member's energy to form a group meta-energy, and the behaviours and decisions of the group become functions of the energy. The members of the group create a single body with their energy and move toward the achievement of a unified goal – i.e., growth and advancement. Most people are well aware of the following verses by Saadi and recite them every day as a way to emphasise the significance of sympathy, cooperation, and collaboration:

Human beings are members of a whole,

in the creation of one essence and soul.

If one member is afflicted with pain,

other members uneasy will remain.

Now, look at the above verses from the perspective of the group energy. They argue that the energy of one member influences that of other members. If an energy-drainer arrives in a group, the person can devour others' energies. On the other hand, if an energiser enters the group, the overall energy of the group increases. Thus, the constructive effects of a group much exceed the situation in which the same task is carried out individually. However, this also holds true for the destructive effects of group work compared to individuals.

Suppose that two farmers dispute the ownership of a piece of land, and the negative effects of the dispute influence their families and themselves. If two clans dispute the ownership of a piece of land, it means the destructive group forces of the two clans oppose one another. During the ancient wars between clans or modern civil or trans-border wars, each person's energy is added to a collector current of energy and influences the output.

The group energy needs to be managed

The group energy needs to be managed so that the power of the group energy can improve the performance of a group. Similar to the case when you manage the energies of the magician inside yourself, you need to manage the group energy of the group when you are dealing with a group. Group managers are not the sole party responsible for enhancing the energy of the group, and every single member has to play a certain role and carry out some responsibilities.

You have two ways to manage the energy of a group and improve its performance:

First, you need to acquire the skills required to carry out successful teamwork and transfer them to other members so that they may eliminate anything that is peripheral and irrelevant from their work.

Second, you should act according to the 20-80 Law, which states that you need to increase your energy level of them to enhance your performance. That is because increasing the energy level of the team by 20% solves 80% of the problems and improves group performance.

Managerial experiences have shown me that if you want to utilise classic methods like training your personnel in teamwork skills or implementing legal procedures to solve the issues of your organisation, you need to spend 80% energy so that you may achieve your desired goals. However, if you try to increase your groupmates' energy levels, the issues will be resolved automatically. This requires you to spend only 20% of your energy. Sometimes when you fail, it is useful to implement some creative ideas to alleviate the spirit of failure and sorrow and increase the energy of the group.

In a group in which energy levels are high, each member believes that he/she is responsible for maintaining or enhancing the energy level of the team or performing more conveniently in their positions or roles. When the energy level of a group increases, you can have a successful team and achieve desirable outcomes. If you are the leader of a group, assess and understand the energy level of each member. Try to understand the position of each member toward his/her responsibility. Observe the manner of their interactions to achieve the most convenient position required to maximise the energy levels of individuals, and then, the whole group.

It is not always the responsibility of managers to make good decisions as some members may show not willing to implement them. That is because such incidents reduce the energy level of the group. Sometimes, a wrong decision that increases the energy levels of the group members can bring about better results.

Boosting the group energy

When the magic of group energy flows through a team, it should be boosted constantly so that it can always maintain the best levels.

In your opinion, how can you increase the group energy of a team?

The members of a group form a unified body; thus, each team has a unique DNA. As a result, its energy drainers and energisers need to be identified, and it should be endeavoured to improve its energy levels. The following five considerations need to be scrutinised to boost the group energy:

1. Do not perform repetitive methods

Repeating the same old methods reduces energy levels. Even when an accurate strategy or decision that increases energy levels gets repeated many times, it will reduce energy every time it is repeated again. Novel endeavours, strategies, decisions, encouragement, punishment, fresh behaviours, and creative ideas are the generators of energy in an institution.

2. Increase the number of energy-giving employees and eliminate the energy-drainers in the group

Maintain equilibrium between energy-drainers and energisers – i.e., the energy seesaw. On the way to create the group energy and maintain the balance between people, we should know that some people are energisers (transfer energy to other people) and some others directly depend on the energy levels of the group (i.e., they are energetic when they energy levels of the environment are high and vice versa). There is also a third group of people who consume the energy of the people around them in any case. They are human energy drainers and include fearful, pessimistic, and hopeless people, in addition to the ones that cannot maintain convenient interactions with their acquaintances.

In any team, young and optimistic members whose energy levels exceed that of others are the energisers of the group. Their energy is not a function of their experiences, knowledge, or skills. They may make mistakes, but they have enough energy to stand again and continue their paths. Young members are more courageous and bolder, have fewer fears of losing, and consider everything novel and amazing. They move headlong toward success. Moreover, each group should contain older and more experienced members whose experiences and skills are valuable for the younger groupmates. Many issues are resolved by such experiences and skills. The older members can pave the way for the energy of the youth by detecting the probable challenges and damages, though they typically have lower energy levels. The two classes can complement one another if they are placed in convenient combinations. The best combination for a successful institution is one that consists of younger members along with more experienced and patient members with sufficient power and patience to work with the former.

3. There is nothing called the right or wrong decision

Any decision, strategy, and behaviour that can increase the energy level of a group according to the group DNA are acceptable. According to the first theorem, what is important is being novel and fresh and not being right or wrong. Then, you should concentrate on novelty as it can increase people's enthusiasm and motivation in groups. If the enthusiasm and motivation of every single member of a group increase, the group energy can be focused on achieving a shared goal. In this way, the energy level of the group gets improved.

Increase people's awareness about their joint work so that the group belief in performing a certain job and achieving the desired outcome can enhance the group energy. Failures are insights to success, according to a group that believes in development and advancement; they believe that each failure breaks down the repository of the energy magicians' hidden energies and activates the super-magic of the group energy.

4. Change and replace people, positions, and methods

Change positions among the members from time to time to change their energy levels. Engage people in their new roles so that they may endeavour to carry them out. That is because changing roles can remove the sense of indolence in people used to their former positions. However, take note that when any promotion or replacement is carried out at the appropriate time or place, it may reduce the group energy instead of increasing it.

5. Challenge the group

An energetic manager who always gives energy to his/her group is not always affable and smiling;

sometimes, she/he may be serious and hard to please! Such managers challenge their team members and place them in risky conditions, expect them to perform something that exceeds their capabilities, and put them in utter discomfort. Moreover, they let the members make mistakes and fail. Such people increase the energy of the group incrementally.

6. The energy domino

The colourful pieces of domino are arranged regularly according to particular rules, and the arrangement results in the creation of a pattern. The untouched pieces are stable, but the most insignificant push by a fingertip is enough to collapse the pieces successively and crash the whole pattern. The energy-transferring behaviours act like dominoes in both positive and negative modes. The first stroke gets transferred into the following pieces, and this may continue until the last piece. You can construct a domino to transfer the group energy so that by increasing the energy of the first person by 5%, you may have the same 5% in the last member. To achieve this goal, you need to make sure that the transfer of energy is not disturbed at any point on the path. Energy drainers stop the movement of the energy dominos. Take good care of your group energy domino to increase the energy.

Remember that the leader of a team is not the one with higher positions and ranks. The real leader is the person who supplies the energy of the group and feeds it with his/her own energy.

Imagine the CEO of a company with six employees. The personnel of the company are working together like the pieces of a domino and are in utmost stability. One day, the manager asked himself, "How can I increase the energy of the organisation?" Then, he makes a strange and unexpected decision. He disturbs the balance of the domino and assigns new responsibilities to each employee to motivate them. The movement of the first person stimulates movement in others. The CEO has upset the preliminary pattern of the domino. If each piece transfers only 5% of the energy to the next piece, the yield of the personnel can reach 30% every day due to the new decision. What significant growth! Is it not a remarkable outcome for a working day?

An interesting step that can be taken by a CEO is to stop acting according to old clichés. This means that you should put aside old habits and do something that has not yet been imagined by another person. Doing something – halting the performance of things according to clichés, or assigning new responsibilities to the members of a group – are instances of the above suggestion in energy management. Getting out of habits in everyday decisions introduces novelty to the monotonous and boring order of an environment and creates energy.

If you hold numerous meetings for a certain project and discuss it for hours on end with no success, try playing a game to increase the energy of your employees to carry out the project. Moreover, perhaps it is better to have fun with your colleagues and then start your work. The fun can act as the insignificant stroke on the first piece of a domino set. In this way, energy flows continuously, and a network of fresh energies gets established.

Do not ignore small interesting actions.

All group members should always think about their share in increasing the group energy of the group

Moreover, a group manager should know that the presence of energisers multiplies the dynamicity of the group toward the achievement of their goals.

The golden rule

Continuity is important to achieve your goals in any endeavour. An attractive idea may face various shortcomings, obstacles, and issues during the implementation phase and no longer look as attractive. You need to be equipped with a rule to stay strong against such difficulties; it is a golden rule that acts like the symbol of an eagle on old treasure maps.

What does the golden rule say?

Continuously spend energy for five years without getting tired.

If you exercise for an hour every day, you just spend four percent of your daily time.

If exercising becomes a fixed part of your days, what changes can you observe in your body after a year? Yes, you will definitely have a healthy and fit body. You need to introduce the same perseverance and consistency into your work – i.e., work for eight hours a day to fulfill your goals. Is it not possible to revolutionise your business? No doubt, your mental and thinking powers get highly sophisticated, and you exercise more control over your affairs! The first five years in any job bring about a minimum of outcomes. The first five years mean perseverance and consistency. Achievements during the period are negligible, but they become more highlighted from the sixth year on. Thus, you prosper during the second six-year period of your work.

The main point is to hold on to the Golden Five-Year Rule.

Many years ago, we started exporting polymer materials and continued it by representing dry cell battery companies. Moreover, we did some time working in the field of clothing and then worked in producing and importing polyurethane, and later, in performing contractual insulation work. Then, we started selling tar. We decided to produce, and this has continued so far. If I am asked questions about the most significant period in my career, I will certainly answer the first five years: the period that had not the least relevance for the current agenda of the company.

Though the period bore no fruit, I still consider it the main reason to attain the present status. Any endeavour that we made during the first five years produced very small outcomes. Our income was not enough to cover bank loan interests, let alone enable us to pay back the company's debts. However, any outcome can be achieved by spending energy over time. We worked tirelessly for five years and struggled with the debts until we made a significant amount of money in the fifth year, which is equal to the total endeavour we had made during the preceding four years. Then, our revenues in the sixth year exceeded the amount of money we had made during the past five years, and this trend has continued until the present moment. A while ago, when I had a session with two very hard-working executives of the company, I told them, "Never think about how much your salary is today; no doubt, you will shine like stars during the next five years. That is because I can see that you are not concerned with your salaries. You are interested in your work and spend energy on it like lovers. This energy will bring about great success for you at the most convenient time." If you spend too much energy without getting the expected outcomes, you should not conclude that your work is wrong! If you persist in your work, you will experience remarkable outcomes in due time.

Energy certainly provides good results.

When you behave according to the Golden Five-Year Rule, it means you spend energy on your work without expecting any outcome. Rest assured that your energy is not wasted at all! Rather, it is transferred to the second five-year period so that you experience incremental success in your work.

The tale of the energy castle

At the end of the present chapter, the significance of group energy and its magical results, which can lead to the destiny of a society and change it, will be discussed again; group energy plays a significant role in the process of human life. The influential and historical role of group energy in human societies in the form of revolutions, wars, reforms, and changes in laws is undeniable.

Once upon a time, there was a castle at the end of the world with three white walls and three gates. The fourth wall was a black one with no gate or window and had the tallest tower watched by five able-bodied guards. The guard changed positions in three-hour intervals. It was said that the guards protected the world against creatures who were called energy drainers. The commanders of the caste constantly warned the guards that, "If you like your families to have energetic and prosperous lives, you need to stick together." They recommended that men maintain higher levels of energy. "If you see an unknown creature that reduced your energy, immediately inform us so that we can go and fight it and save the castle and the world from the possibility of destruction."

The tale says that the period was the golden era of human life. Very high levels of energy flew everywhere, and everybody endeavoured to grow and advance themselves and their groups. The golden five-year rule was always observed, and people grew according to it. Everyone's life was desirable and satisfactory. Elders, commanders, and soldiers in that land pursued a shared goal: they sought to maintain the golden age and the beautiful flow of energy. The commanders and elders who had stayed in the castle for many years would say, "When you fight those energy drainers, form a strong and unbreakable chain; if anyone feels weak during the struggle, another person should replace him so that the energy domino may not break down." It had been foretold that if the energy domino of the castle failed, the whole world would change drastically.

According to this quoted history of the castle, it had been documented that when the ancient ancestors constructed the place, the fourth wall was also made of white stone and a walnut gate. Moreover, the people lived with no pain or suffering alongside one another in the castle. The people were free of any feeling of ownership, regret, comparison, fear of failure, and hopelessness, and everybody utilised their energy to achieve their desires and goals. However, one day, a tiny creature entered the castle through the walnut gate. A small boy who was playing nearby saw the creature and held it in his hand. The creature bit his hand. The boy screamed and dropped it on the ground, but the creature got a bit bigger! The unhappy and angry boy kicked the creature, but it bit his toes. The boy grabbed a pebble, but the strange creature had disappeared. The boy went to inform the older ones and showed them his wounded finger. Everybody gathered to find the strange creature, but the search was futile! Some people accused the boy of lying, while others took his side and pointed to the wound on his finger.

Still, others thought that a boy should not be so fearful and soft to instigate such a commotion only because of a small creature. The people started to seriously disagree with each other, and they could not agree on anything from that day on. They frowned and fretted at each other. Suddenly, they saw a very strange black giant with its youngsters, and no one dared to get closer to them. The babies quickly grew and became more powerful. Since their arrival, feelings of greed, ownership, jealousy, the fear of loss, and many other feelings became more highlighted, and no one was satisfied with their lives anymore. Moreover, people's energy levels dropped constantly. The people feared the creatures and did not remember how to stick together. They no longer remembered how to connect their energies, and this caused those strange creatures to ruin the beautiful castle in the early days of the world. The survivors who were hiding in a cave reached a conclusion; instead of continuing their disagreements, they needed to establish an energy domino and fight the creatures. They promised that they would support each other and not be scared of anything. Even if they failed, they would turn the very failure into a source of energy and fight with the energy-eating creatures.

In this way, they waged war against the energy drainers and gave each other energy by saying that they would rebuild the castle and make it prosperous again. They started to understand that whenever they supported each other and remembered the purpose of their fight, the creatures became frightened and smaller in size. They tended to become weaker as the energy levels of the people accompanying them went up. The fighters understood how to protect their energy domino. The energy drainers, which had become enervated due to the power of the group energy, saw no other way to leave. Then, the victorious people repaired the white wall and sealed the gate with stone and mortar. They installed a plaque on the wall and wrote on it, "Be careful of energy drainers. If you want to become stronger, you need to get connected to the group energy of your group. If we are together, no energy drainer can penetrate our stronghold."

In the end, they added, "The group energy is a huge and powerful one." In sum, the castle remained for countless years at the end of the world to protect our world, though no one knows anything about its fate! There are numerous stories about the end of the castle. According to one, all territories were discovered, and the population of humans got increased. Then, the population of energy drainers increased, and all of them attacked the ancient castle at the end of the world. This time, the castle could not resist and was ruined forever. Another story claims that the castle is still intact and appears in different shapes in various places on the earth due to an ancient spell – i.e., perhaps in the form of an energetic sports team that wins the Olympic Games, an internal band, a highly successful commercial corporation, or a book titled "The Magic of Energy." Who knows? No matter how the castle appears, its gift – the magic of energy – will be with us forever.

Dear reader, now you are well informed of the magic of group energy described in the present work, and you have been summoned to make great leaps toward success in your life. Then, bring about the most in your life after finishing the book.

Afterword

The reason for writing the present book was that years of endeavouring and doing trial and error had endowed me with attitudes and thoughts that could not be found in any inspirational or personal development books. It was a fresh and original concept that enabled me to look at everything in a special and different way.

Achieving such an attitude acts like magical glasses. A new meaning and interpretation can be gained by looking at everything using the energy glasses. Moreover, it can be used to evaluate your hidden internal energy. This makes it possible to quickly and accurately detect energisers and energy drainers, and the detection of the two is the most significant instrument to manage the magical energy so that it can utilise its powerful spells and direct our internal energies toward the right path.

Such an attitude helped me to discover the miracle of "starting" and "failing and risking", which acted as super-energisers and created powerful energies. On the other hand, I found the energy-draining nature of concepts like "success," "perfectionism," and "the sense of possession" – to name but a few, which could act as a black hole and devour all or a significant portion of our energy. By revealing such secrets and their functions in our lives and businesses, I gradually learned how to counteract the black holes and protect the magical energy.

I understood that if I intended to upgrade my level of life, first, I needed to accept that "gaining more" in most cases could not enhance energy levels, and "losing" did not necessarily mean the loss of energy. Then, I paid attention to my energy levels instead of concentrating on what I had and lacked and my level of life.

I made a start. I experienced significant losses and gained significant energy from them. I took risks and started again. I moved forward constantly and tirelessly as I believed in the law of energy conservation. I was certain that if I spent energy on something and did not achieve the desired outcome, the energy remained in me forever and returned to me at another time and place. That was because energy is always the most significant factor since energy is the main factor, and the rest are peripheral matters.

If I am asked, "What is your most significant possession?" I will no doubt point to my "internal energy." I wrote this book so that it may elucidate a new level of understanding and create (though small) changes in the readers' attitudes. However, I should add that the present book sheds light on the road that has taken me to the present point and needs to be completed in upcoming editions with more novel opinions. Thus, though reading the book is over now, the book of the magic of energy is still open, and you can create your own story by taking novel attitudes toward the concept of energy; that is because, as I argued before, people can have different experiences and ways of achieving success, and no two individuals pass the same road in an exactly similar way.

Then, do not wait for invitations, the right condition, or others' help to take your first step. Merely taking the first step opens new doors to you and provides you with new chances and opportunities.

I wish you great losses for you so that you can take risks, start again, and take more significant steps afterward.

Dear reader, if you renewed motivation and enthusiasm to start and work, the book has fulfilled its responsibility. Now, you can introduce it to your friends who are looking for transformation and share any effects that you felt by reading it. In this way, all of us will be linked together by the process of energy exchange and will maximally use the magic of the group energy to grow and transcend.

Move ahead

Like a river that flows headlong toward the stone in a steep valley

Live long

As no miracle can be expected of the dead.

Stay energetic, dynamic, and pioneering.

Mohammad Mahdi Dousti

Tehran, Spring 2022

www.ingramcontent.com/pod-product-compliance
Lightning Source LLC
Chambersburg PA
CBHW030828090426
42737CB00009B/917